The World of Pleasure

The Grand Tour

The World of Pleasure

Flavio Conti

Translated by Patrick Creagh

Cassell
London

CASSELL LTD.
35 Red Lion Square, London WC1R 4SG
and at Sydney, Auckland, Toronto, Johannesburg,
an affiliate of
Macmillan Publishing Co., Inc.,
New York

First published in Great Britain 1979

ISBN 0 304 30021 7

Printed in Hong Kong by Mandarin Publishers Limited

Photography Credits:
Aerofilms: pp. 10–11 / *Borromeo:* pp. 121–124, p. 125 right,
top, and bottom, p. 127 top, center, and bottom left, pp.
128–132 / *British Tourist Authority:* p. 27 bottom left /
Cauchetier: pp. 137–148, pp. 154–156, p. 157 center and
bottom, p. 158 top left and bottom, pp. 159–161 / *Costa:* p.
108 right, p. 109 center, pp. 110–113, p. 116 / *Hassia:* p. 9, p.
14 bottom, p. 15 left and top right, p. 18, p. 19 top right and
bottom left and right, p. 31 bottom / *Hassmann:* pp. 57–68,
pp. 73–96 / *Hornak:* p. 12, p. 13 top, p. 14 top left and right,
p. 15 bottom right, p. 21 left, pp. 29–30 / *Interfoto-Scholz:*
p. 44 bottom / *Kersting:* p. 28 top, p. 32 / *Lazzeri:* p. 125
left, p. 127 bottom right / *Manuscina:* pp. 42–43, p. 44 top,
p. 45 bottom, p. 46 bottom left, center, and right, p. 47, p. 48
top, p. 49 top and bottom left, pp. 50–51 / *Novosti:* p. 46
top, p. 48 bottom left / *Rizzoli P.:* pp. 106–107 / *Radici:* p.
108 top and bottom left, p. 109 top and bottom, pp. 114–115
/ *S.E.F.:* p. 41, p. 45 top, p. 48 bottom right, p. 49 center left
and top and bottom right, p. 52, p. 105 / *Sheridan:* p. 13
bottom, pp. 16–17, p. 19 top left, p. 20, p. 21 top and bottom
right, p. 28 bottom left and right, p. 31 top, p. 153, p. 157
top, p. 158 top right, pp. 162–164 / *U.K. Department of
Environment:* pp. 22–26, p. 27 top and bottom right.

Rizzoli Editore

Authors of the Italian Edition: Dr. Flavio Conti,
  Gianfranco Malafarina, G. M. Tabarelli
Idea and Realization, Harry C. Lindinger
General Supervisor, Luigi U. Re
Graphic Designer, Gerry Valsecchi
Coordinator, Vilma Maggioni
Editorial Supervisor, Gianfranco Malafarina
Research Organizer, Germano Facetti
U.S. Edition Coordinator, Natalie Danesi
  Murray

Contents

Preface

The World of Pleasure

One does not have to be a philosopher to realize that it is more fun to work at enjoying life rather than to spend one's life working. The true business of living is not adding up columns of figures, or selling encyclopedias, or doing any of the thousand-and-one jobs by which people earn their living. It is, instead, learning to appreciate the things money cannot buy, such as enjoying one's friends, strolling and chatting, and reveling in nature and fresh air. *Carpe diem*—seize the day—the poet enjoins.

Not everyone, of course, has the means to follow this advice. Unfortunately, many leisure activities demand money and time as well as a certain education and curiosity. A pleasant and congenial environment also makes a major difference. The powerful, the aristocratic, and the wealthy of all nations and epochs have always recognized the delight of a luxurious residence and have often built themselves palatial retreats in which to relax and get away from it all. Despite the common denominators of comfort and often ostentatious privacy, these monuments vary considerably. They mirror the penchants and whims of powerful and opinionated men and women who could afford to build anything they wished.

The Italians of the Renaissance discovered and perfected the civilized pleasures of gracious homes. They called their leisure residences *"luoghi di delizie"*—places of delight—beautiful villas set in well-kept grounds, amply spacious and conspicuously comfortable. In German, the name for such resplendent homes was *Lustschloss*, or pleasure palace. Early in the seventeenth century, the powerful archbishop of Salzburg, Wolfdietrich von Raitenau, built such a palace on the outskirts of the city for his mistress Salome Alt and their fifteen children. Schloss Altenau, as it was called (for von Raitenau succeeded in having Salome elevated to the nobility and her name changed to Salome von Altenau) was a splendid Italian-style villa.

But Salome was unable to enjoy her fine home on the bank of the River Salzach for long. Von Raitenau's political fortunes declined abruptly, and the palace (rechristened Mirabell) became the summer residence of succeeding archbishops. Two of Austria's most famous architects worked on the palace. Fischer von Erlach is thought to have designed the Baroque garden, and Lucas von Hildebrandt renovated the building itself. But in 1818, a great fire all but destroyed the palace. It was rebuilt soon after, and Salome Alt's Lustschloss now serves as Salzburg's municipal offices.

A second German pleasure palace in this volume is the palace of Sanssouci at Potsdam, which was designed and built by Frederick the Great of Prussia. Frederick was a brilliant military leader who preferred to spend his time amid music and learned conversation with the most remarkable and cultured minds of his time. Voltaire once called him "the philosopher-king." Frederick himself chose the site for Sanssouci—meaning "without care"—and drew up his own plans for the summer residence. He refused to give in to his architect's wishes for a grander palace befitting the powerful sovereign. Frederick instead insisted on a single-story building, so that he could walk directly out onto his grounds.

Sanssouci is set discreetly on a low-lying hill. Below it, six tiers of flowing stairs and terraces of greenhouses for grapes and exotic fruits slope down to a lively fountain. Within, the rooms of the palace are formal and tastefully decorated. Frederick delighted in Sanssouci, and at the age of seventy-four ended his days there. Sadly enough, his desire to be buried in the tomb he had prepared on the topmost terrace of his garden was not honored, as it was considered beneath his dignity as a king.

By contrast, the palace of the maharanahs of Udaipur, in the state of Rajasthan, northern India, is monumentally grand. In 1567, in the face of the Mogul invasions, the *rana* (maharanahs) of

Mewar fled the city of Chitor and founded the beautiful city of Udaipur, high in the Aravalli hills. The original unadorned rana's palace, overlooking shimmering Lake Pichola, has been enlarged and embellished over the centuries, becoming more delicate and refined with each addition. Moslem and Indian styles are juxtaposed and blended. The turrets, kiosks, and pavilions of northern India exist alongside the domes, arches, enameled tiles, and oriel windows of Moslem architecture. Lattices and trellised balconies characterize the façade of the women's quarters. The white complex of buildings, shining under the still Indian sky, appeals to the senses with its evocation of calmness, luxury, and languorous opulence.

Like the palace of Udaipur, the palace of Petrodvorets, on the outskirts of Leningrad, was built by the founder of the city. Having successfully defeated the Swedes in the Great Northern War, Peter the Great of Russia decided to consolidate his position as master of the Baltic by founding a city on the Gulf of Finland. St. Petersburg, as it was named, became Russia's "window on Europe" and Peterhof—"Peter's house"—his European-style summer residence. Peter hired a French architect to design the palace and elaborate gardens, with their myriad fountains—including many which surprised visitors by squirting them with jets of water from artificial trees and shrubs. The palace remained the favorite of succeeding Romanov rulers, including Peter's daughter Elizabeth who reshaped the gardens in the Russian Rococo style and Catherine the Great who entertained her many lovers in the pavilion of Monplaisir on the grounds.

St. Petersburg is now called Leningrad, after the man who swept the Romanovs from the face of the earth. Peterhof—its name Russianized to Petrodvorets—was devastated and half-demolished by German troops during the long siege of Leningrad in World War II. But it has been meticulously rebuilt and restored. It stands as an eloquent witness to Russia's respect for its historical treasures, al-

though it is now a people's park, providing pleasure for the many instead of the few.

In a sense, the palace of Hampton Court took the opposite path, passing from a commoner, Cardinal Wolsey, to his sovereign, Henry VIII. After spending a fortune making his residence the most modern and spacious in England and embellishing it with exotic works of art, the cardinal found himself obliged to make a gift of the palace to his autocratic king who had taken a fancy to it. Wolsey's loyalty did not get him far, however. When he failed to obtain a divorce for the king, Henry had him arrested and then charged him with high treason.

A long line of British monarchs made Hampton Court their home, each leaving their mark on the house and grounds and amassing a priceless collection of paintings by Holbein and many masters of the Italian Renaissance. But in the nineteenth century, Queen Victoria turned the pleasure palace over to the people, so that now everyone can enjoy the landscaping by Le Nôtre, the exotic plants and Dutch gardens of Mary II, the wings built by Sir Christopher Wren, and the famous maze.

On quite a different scale from Hampton Court with its 1,000 rooms is the chateau of Azay-le-Rideau. This mansion was one of the earliest of those which gracefully dot the Loire Valley region of France. Originally, it was a medieval fortress built by the knight Hugues-le-Ridel to defend the area from the English. This first structure was burned down, but from its ruins there rose the graceful Renaissance country chateau which still stands. Built by the artistic and cultivated treasurer general of France and his wife, the castle seems an ethereal and enchanted vision. It stands with one of its two wings built out over the placid waters of the Indre, its Gothic turrets adding an air of further unreality to this peaceful residence. Philippe Lesbahy and her husband never got to enjoy their new home, however. Before it was completed, they were forced to flee France after being implicated in a political scandal. Today it can be enjoyed by all as it is now a state-owned

museum of Renaissance furnishings.

Architectural luxuries are not limited to private homes and palaces. Today the coasts of the world are lined with towns and villages whose sole raison d'être is to provide accommodation and fun for holiday makers. The town of Deauville on the Norman coast of France is one such resort. It is still fashionable, although in a far more subdued way than during its two heydays of the belle époque and the Roaring Twenties. Then, aristocrats, millionaires, and their retinues would flock to Deauville to spend the season yachting, horse racing, and being conspicuously indolent at all times.

The symbolic heart of the town is the casino, where magnates and moneyed sophisticates flaunt their wealth by winning or losing vast sums with indifference. An unassuming building, somewhat academic in style, the casino has played host to many of the richest and most glamorous personalities of the century. It also fascinates the less rich with its mildly decadent but still powerful allure.

It may seem strange to include among these pleasure palaces a flight of stairs, but the Spanish Steps in Rome well deserve their place in this volume. These golden travertine steps, built in the eighteenth century, attracted bohemians, artists, and intellectuals of all nationalities throughout the nineteenth century. Today on the broad terraces, artists and flower sellers display their wares, and students and tourists meet and watch the world go by. The character of the steps, and the Piazza di Spagna below, is inimitably Roman—at once intimate and grandiose, fusing several different experiences into one. The richness of the Baroque, overarched by the warm Roman sky, is molded into spaces in which humans can meet, walk, and talk with comfort and enjoyment—an open-air pleasure palace.

Meeting, walking, and talking are among the true delights of life. And memorable architecture provides people with a space in which to enjoy those pleasures.

Hampton Court Palace

England

Hampton Court (preceding page), the pleasure palace associated with every English monarch from Henry VIII to George III, was built in 1515 by Cardinal Thomas Wolsey as his private residence. In 1529, after Wolsey had failed to arrange Henry VIII's divorce from Catherine of Aragon, the king seized the palace for his own use. Today the eight-acre complex, fourteen miles up the River Thames from London, encompasses old Tudor courtyards and two massive Baroque wings designed by Sir Christopher Wren (1632–1723). Wren spent forty-eight years attempting to transform the palace into a "Versailles-on-the-Thames."

The approach to Hampton Court from the Thames is guarded by Wolsey's Great West Gatehouse (above left). This structure was once much larger and more imposing, but George III lopped off the two top stories to avoid paying for their repair. Nineteenth-century renovations of the gatehouse (above right) are noticeable because the red Victorian brick used contrasts strongly with the original, almost purple Tudor brickwork. Henry lined the entrance to the gatehouse with heraldic lions, dragons, leopards, and hounds (below right) to celebrate his acquisition of the palace he had coveted for over a decade. The king also removed Wolsey's coat of arms from the central oriel window and replaced it with his own. The Italian Renaissance terracotta medallions of Roman emperors on the side turrets were erected by Wolsey, attesting to his receptivity to more modern influences.

The Base Court (below left), largest of Hampton Court's thirteen inner courtyards, is connected by the Clock Court tower to a smaller inner quadrangle surrounded by Wolsey's private apartments. When Henry moved into the palace with his bride-to-be, Anne Boleyn, he ordered the royal monograms A and H—entwined in a true lovers' knot—displayed throughout the courtyards. Four years later, Anne was executed and her initials were removed. For some reason, the monograms on the ceiling of this portal were overlooked, and it has been known ever since as Anne Boleyn's Gate.

The Lion Gate (above left) was installed in the early eighteenth century by Queen Anne, the last Stuart monarch. Like the prancing unicorn on the main gateway to the palace (above far right), this is a later addition to the menagerie of heraldic beasts. The hound holding a coat of arms of Richard I (below far right) was one of Henry's first contributions to his new palace.

Hampton Court's moat (below) was among the last to be dug in England. It was originally crossed by a wooden bridge, which Henry replaced with the present heraldic stone one. This medieval defense is overlooked by terra-cotta medallions characteristic of the Italian Renaissance. More typically Tudor are the oriel window (near right) and ornamental brickwork chimneys (above right).

Preceding page, the east façade of Hampton Court which houses the Queen's Staterooms. Its central pediment (top right) displays a relief sculpted by Caius Gabriel Cibber, depicting "Hercules's Triumph over Envy," a fitting subject for a project that was motivated by King William III's rivalry with the Sun King. Below, two emblematic carvings from the façade of the King's Staterooms: center, a martial trophy above the central door; bottom, the royal coat of arms of William and Mary.

The symmetry and repetition of Wren's south façade (facing page) give an impression of magnificence and power. Wren's façade contrasts with the freer design of Cardinal Wolsey's Tudor palace built almost 200 years earlier. The central portico of the south façade (above) marks the large Audience Hall. Above right, the southwest corner of the palace where Wren's new wing joins the old Tudor walls, with their patterned brickwork, distinctive oriel windows, and ornamental turrets.

Below near right, Mars, god of war, standing guard over the entrance to the King's Apartments. Below far right, one of the vases on the terrace in front of the south façade.

*Contrasting views of Hampton Court's Tudor and Baroque courtyards:
Henry VIII's Great Hall (above) looms above the grassy quadrangle of
the Base Court. The Clock Court (below), from which the hall is entered,
is named for the remarkable tower clock created by Nicholas Oursian in
1540. The clock tells the month, the position of the sun in the ecliptic, the
phases of the moon, and even the time of high water at London Bridge.*

Wren's Fountain Court (left, above, and below) replaced Henry VIII's private apartments on the so-called Cloister Green Court. In the late seventeenth century, Wren's repetitive use of sash windows, rather than casements, was the height of modernity.

Henry VIII's Great Hall (left) is best known for its magnificent hammer-beam ceiling, highlighted throughout in gold. The tapestries, whose overall length reaches 826 yards, are original. The heraldic stained-glass windows, however, are nineteenth-century replacements. In this room, Henry dined in state with his last five wives, Queen Elizabeth I celebrated Christmas, and William Shakespeare probably performed before James I.

Cardinal Wolsey's Chapel Royal (right), which has been remodeled twice, is also famous for its ceiling. The intricate gilt and blue vault, decorated with pendants and trumpeting cherubs, is all that remains of Henry VIII's contributions. Christopher Wren installed the floor, wood pews, and the towering Classical reredos behind the altar, which was carved by Grinling Gibbons. Above, an ornate fireplace crowned by a bust of Venus in the Queen's Gallery. The work of John Nost, this piece was made for Queen Mary (1689–1694).

Tudor cooks could roast an entire ox in the eighteen-foot-long hearth of the kitchen at Hampton Court (following page). The photograph shows less than a third of the enormous room, which is itself part of a much larger complex. Surviving equipment, such as the portable braziers, offers a fascinating glimpse of Tudor domestic life.

Breathtaking in scale if not universally admired, the King's Staircase (above and near right) was designed by Christopher Wren for King William III. The wrought-iron bannister is the work of the French artist Jean Tijou. The murals, depicting Roman gods at play, are by the court painter Antonio Verrio. In a vain attempt to recover money owed him for this work, Verrio later painted the ceiling of Queen Anne's drawing room (above far right), characterizing Anne as the spirit of Justice. Anne undoubtedly understood Verrio's intentions but did not settle the debts incurred by her brother-in-law William. The queen's drawing room (left) is typical of the interiors of the newer wings of Hampton Court.

Painted by Sir James Thornhill, the ceiling of Queen Anne's bedroom (below far right) portrays "Rosy-Fingered Aurora" preparing to lead the Sun's chariot on its daily course.

The grounds of Hampton Court reflect the enthusiasm shown by many of the palace's royal tenants for the gardens and display the evolution of landscaping over two and a half centuries. Above and below right, geometric flower beds, formal lawns, and straight rows of lime trees—the hallmark of the Great Fountain Garden. This expansive, Baroque garden was laid out during the reign of Charles II after plans by the French gardener Le Nôtre and was completed by Mary II, an admirer of Dutch gardens. The enclosure (below left) was originally planted by Cardinal Wolsey, who was primarily interested in growing herbs and vegetables.

Henry VIII's colorful Pond Garden (right) includes sculpted shrubs and a great variety of flowers typically found in English gardens.

Above, the medieval Knot Garden with its intricate design of flowers and low shrubs. Wolsey included a garden with this same pattern in his original plans for Hampton Court. Below left, one of the three narrow alleys, decorated with statuary, which cut through the trees and tall shrubs of the Privy Garden between the palace and the Thames. At the river entrance to this garden is the Tijou Screen (below right), a wrought-iron fence designed for Mary II by Jean Tijou.

Above right, William III's Banqueting Hall, built in 1700, seen behind Henry VIII's Pond Garden. Here William could entertain his coterie of male favorites in privacy.

Many exotic and rare plants, collected by English monarchs over the years, are preserved in the palace greenhouses. The most famous is the Great Vine (right). Planted in 1758, it yields about a ton of a rare variety of dark grape each year.

Following page, the Long Canal, an artificial waterway in Hampton Court's outer park. Four hundred and fifty years ago, Henry VIII hunted stags in the palace grounds. Today, the park is an oasis located within easy reach of the heart of London.

Hampton Court Palace England

The King's court
Should have the excellence;
But Hampton Court
Hath the pre-eminence.

In January 1515, when Thomas Wolsey took possession of the manor of Hampton Court and set out to turn it into England's most palatial residence, it was inevitable that the project would become the target of jibes like that penned by the poet John Skelton. Wolsey had been named archbishop of York only a few months before and was destined for a cardinal's hat be-

fore the year was out. Soon thereafter, he would become Lord Chancellor of the realm and holder of several of the country's richest bishoprics.

It was particularly galling for well-born courtiers to watch this butcher's son surpass them in wealth and influence with the young King Henry VIII. In foreign affairs, Wolsey's power was so great that in 1517 an Italian visitor wrote: "The King pays the Cardinal such respect that he speaks only through his [Wolsey's] mouth." Nevertheless, Wolsey was careful to make it known that Hampton Court was not for his personal enjoyment, claiming that the palace was necessary as an impressive setting for his diplomatic negotiations. However, during the very years when Wolsey was spending a fortune on Hampton Court, Henry's palace at Westminster had been badly damaged by fire, and he and his court spent many months moving about the country and taking advantage of the hospitality of one noble family after another. Eventually it became all too clear to the king that Hampton Court was above all a symbol of Henry's dependence on his most-favored subject.

Meanwhile, just as Wolsey's administrative genius was serving the immediate interests of England, his excellent taste and even his tendency toward hypochondria were creating a palace that was fit not just for one king but for generations of kings and queens. The manor house that Wolsey had obtained was not particularly grand. But it was chosen on behalf of the cardinal by a party of physicians who declared it to be the most salubrious spot within a fourteen-mile radius of London. The doctors' decision proved to be a good one. Hampton Court's freedom from "sweating sickness," plague, and the other diseases rampant in London would serve the English court well for two and a half centuries.

Wolsey began his tenancy by making Hampton Court an even healthier place by installing a plumbing system far ahead of its time. Lead pipes brought fresh water

Below, an old engraving of the plan of the Great Fountain Garden, as it was originally designed—purportedly by Versailles's landscape architect Le Nôtre—for Charles II.

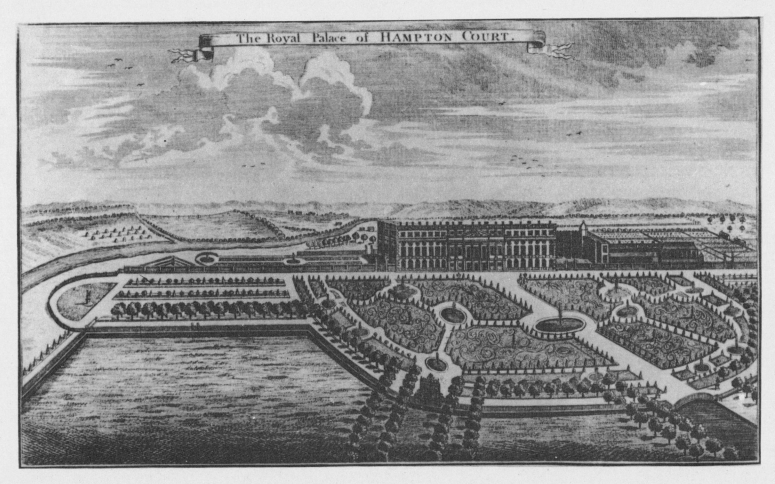

The Royal Palace of HAMPTON COURT.

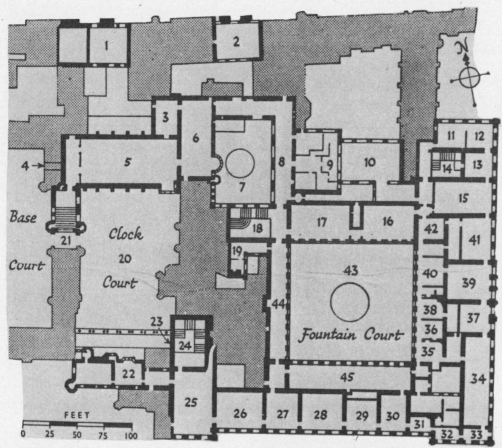

This plan of Hampton Court (above) shows the two principal Tudor courtyards to the left, with Anne Boleyn's Gate (21), the Great Hall (5), the Haunted Gallery (8), and the Chapel Royal (10). Wren's new staterooms, ranged around Fountain Court, include the King's Staircase (24), the Audience Chamber (29), the Queen's Gallery (34), and the Cartoon Gallery (45).

Above, Cardinal Wolsey, portrayed by an unknown sixteenth-century painter. Below, left to right, three of Henry VIII's ill-fated queens: Anne Boleyn and Catherine Howard, both executed for adultery, and Jane Seymour, who died in childbirth.

to the manor from a series of springs over three miles away. Enormous brick sewers, five feet high and three feet wide, carried all sewage directly to the Thames. At the same time, Wolsey had the old house demolished and the entire 2,000-acre estate enclosed by a brick wall. Work on the palace began early in 1515 and proceeded so rapidly that the cardinal was entertaining there a year later.

Wolsey's anonymous architect was quite innovative for his time. Though Hampton Court had a moat, one of the last constructed in England, it otherwise bore little resemblance to the typically dark, heavily walled medieval castles. The palace's 1,000 rooms, including 280 guest bedrooms, space for a domestic staff of over 500, and a stable, were spread out over an area of eight acres. And the plum-red Tudor bricks, mullioned windows, and decorative turrets achieved the combination of regal dignity and spaciousness which impressed foreign dignitaries.

Wolsey spared no expense on the final embellishments of his new palace. In addition to his own unparalleled collection of relics, monstrances, and tapestries with religious themes, he was one of the first Englishmen to appreciate the secular art of the Renaissance. He brought the sculptor Giovanni Maiano from Italy to create a series of terra-cotta medallions portraying Roman emperors for the gatehouses of Base Court and Clock Court, the palace's two most important quadrangles. And he hung the walls of his audience chambers with fine Renaissance tapestries illustrating secular themes.

Although Wolsey argued that none of this magnificence was intended for his own enjoyment, he did not stint on the decoration of his private rooms. In the sections of these apartments that survive today, the original fine oak paneling,

Right, an eighteenth-century view of Christopher Wren's new wing from the formal expanses of the Great Fountain Garden. Below right, four garden pavilions.

carved in a linenfold pattern, can still be seen as can the Renaissance stucco ceilings and friezes. Here the churchman of humble birth walked on Damascene carpets given to him by the doge of Venice, dined in splendor, and slept in a bedstead ornamented with four "Cardinall hattes gilte" and covered with a canopy of red satin.

For fourteen years Wolsey lived in his magnificent manor. But in the summer of 1525, King Henry, who was then his guest, wondered aloud why a butcher's son should live better than he did. Without hesitation, the cardinal replied: "To show how noble a palace a subject may offer to his sovereign." This was exactly what Henry wanted to hear. Wolsey followed up on his remark and transferred the deed of Hampton Court to the Crown. But he delayed moving out, trusting that as long as he was the key to Henry's plans for obtaining a church-approved divorce from his queen, Catherine of Aragon, the issue was unlikely to be raised.

Wolsey had risen far on merit and ambition, but these qualities could not prevent fortune from turning against him eventually. In the summer of 1529, the Holy Roman Emperor, Charles V, a nephew of Queen Catherine, defeated England's French allies in Italy and took the pope prisoner. This was the complete undoing of Wolsey's European strategy, and Henry, who had been waiting thirteen years for his divorce, vented his frustration on his old servant. Wolsey was stripped of all his high offices, apart from one bishopric in the north of England. He died on November 30, 1530, while under arrest for high treason. By that time, Henry and his next bride, Anne Boleyn, were already installed at Hampton Court.

Determined to set his personal stamp on the palace, Henry immediately began extensive renovations. Wolsey's coat of arms

was replaced by the royal insignia, and the old bridge across the moat, adorned with figures representing the struggles of Hercules, was replaced by a stone one guarded by heraldic beasts. While expanding his living quarters, Henry added a new quadrangle known as Cloister Green Court (now destroyed) as well as new kitchens, pantries, butteries, sculleries, sauceries, and wine cellars. He also constructed a bowling alley and a tennis court.

Perhaps Henry's greatest change was the demolition of Wolsey's Great Hall on the south side of Clock Court, which he replaced with a still larger Great Hall, famous for its elaborate Gothic-Tudor ceiling of suspended hammer beams. Like the heraldic beasts on the bridge, this gilded ceiling harked back to medieval taste; however, the completed decorations of the hall reveal the unmistakable influence of the Renaissance.

Henry's Great Hall, which was restored to its original grandeur under the direction of Queen Victoria's consort Prince Albert, may well be the most historic room in England. Here Henry dined in state, not just with Anne Boleyn but with all of his last five queens.

Under Henry's two immediate successors, the Great Hall saw few good times. The regent of his son, Edward VI, was so unpopular that he and the child king had to flee Hampton Court under cover of night. Queen Mary Tudor, daughter of Henry and Catherine of Aragon, spent much of her time at the palace suffering the humiliations of a false pregnancy and an indifferent husband.

Under Henry's second daughter, Elizabeth, the hall truly came into its own. The Virgin Queen traveled extensively, but she considered Hampton Court her home and contributed to its store of rich furnishings—tapestries and tablecloths encrusted with pearls and gems, inlaid tables and writing desks, and exquisite musical instruments. Christmas was the high point of the court year, and the Great Hall became the scene of lavish banquets, masques, and theatrical productions. One of these, a children's pageant known as *The Historie of Error,* is thought to have been the inspiration for Shakespeare's *Comedy of Errors.*

Elizabeth's heirs, James I and his Danish wife Anne, continued to stage plays in the Great Hall. They spared no expense in their productions, hiring the architect Inigo Jones to design scenery and raiding Elizabeth's wardrobe for costumes. Many of their presentations were forgettable pageants written by members of the court, but others were the work of professionals. William Shakespeare himself was an actor in one performance of a play called *Robin Goodfellow.*

The Stuart monarchs (1603–1707) solidified the tradition of using Hampton Court chiefly as a pleasure palace. They used Whitehall Palace in London (another of Wolsey's confiscated mansions) as their primary residence but retired to Hampton Court to enjoy honeymoons, hunting, and romantic dalliances—activities that occupied no small portion of their time.

Aside from their latent Catholicism, the worst flaw of the Stuarts from the English point of view was their contempt for the people they ruled. Charles I, who was no worse than his father James in this respect,

Engravings from the time of George III (1760–1820) show courtiers strolling in the Privy Garden (top) and enjoying the avenues that radiate from Wren's east façade to the Thames (immediately above).

Right, a portrait of Sir Christopher Wren by Godfrey Kneller. Wren was the architect of St. Paul's Cathedral and fifty-one other London churches.

Above, the Broad Walk at Hampton Court, which separates the King's Staterooms from the Great Fountain Garden, as it looked in 1745. The walk was lined with geometrically trimmed yews and imported lime trees.

though more inept and unlucky, was held prisoner at Hampton Court at the end of the English civil war. He escaped from the palace only to be recaptured and, finally, beheaded at Whitehall Palace. Under other circumstances, Charles might have earned a place in history for his genius as an art collector. Although criticized during his lifetime for "squandering. . .millions of Pounds on old, rotten pictures," he acquired most of the finer paintings in the Crown's art collection today—and at bargain prices. Besides commissioning Anthony Van Dyck and Velázquez to produce original works, Charles purchased masterpieces by Titian, Tintoretto, Correggio, and Mantegna. Most of these treasures found their way to Hampton Court.

After Charles's execution in 1649, Parliament decided to sell the palace and its contents in order to pay the Stuart debts. The sale catalogue reflected true Puritan contempt for the trappings of royalty. Fine tapestries, for example, were sold by the yard like so much fustian; several of Titian's best paintings were appraised as if they had been run-of-the-mill portraits.

The rescue of both palace and paintings came in a bizarre turn of events. The dour Oliver Cromwell fell in love with Hampton Court. Much to the shock of Parliament, he moved there with his family. When Parliament sold the land anyway, he bought it back from the new owner, putting the deed in his own name. Far from despising the carnal subjects of the works in Charles's collection, Cromwell moved some of the most entertaining pictures to his own quarters.

When Charles's son returned from exile and assumed the throne, he was more interested in enjoying Hampton Court than

in developing it. He did, however, make considerable efforts to buy back the dispersed treasures and restore the palace as nearly as possible to its former state. At this time the Black Death was sweeping London. All the king's mistresses, favorites, and illegitimate offspring often congregated at healthy Hampton Court.

Into this ménage Charles brought his convent-bred Portuguese bride Catherine and her retinue of chaperones and religious mentors. The new queen was unable to bear children, but fortunately times had changed since the reign of Henry VIII, and Charles was a considerably more easygoing sort. He insisted that Queen Catherine accept the presence of his mistresses but otherwise treated her kindly.

Like almost every resident of Hampton Court, Charles II took an avid interest in the gardens of the estate. In fact, the personalities of each royal owner can be glimpsed in the changes they made to the landscape. Wolsey is best remembered for his medieval Knot Garden, now restored,

Charles II (above far left) lived at Hampton Court during the years of the Great Plague in London. Above near left, William III, the Dutch prince who ruled jointly with his wife, Mary II. His free-spending ways made him unpopular with Parliament.

Both Mary II (below far left) and Queen Anne (below near left) were daughters of the deposed King James II. Anne, who was chronically ill, lost thirteen children, all but one as infants.

the Communications Gallery to view Peter Lely's portraits of the beautiful women of Charles II's court; and they walk through the Orangerie, built as a series of greenhouses, to see Mantegna's nine paintings of the *Triumph of Julius Caesar.*

In most other respects, Wren's project was ill favored. Queen Mary died at the age of thirty-two, without ever living in her new quarters. William was severely criticized by Parliament for spending so much money, and his funds were withdrawn. The aged Christopher Wren, who survived both his patrons, was left struggling to finish the two wings he had begun and to see that the workmen were paid. Finally, in 1718, after serving forty-eight years as surveyor general (during which time he had rebuilt fifty-two of London's churches in the wake of the Great Fire), the eighty-six-year-old architect was summarily dismissed and replaced by a crony of King George I.

Queen Mary left her mark on the royal gardens. Inspired by Dutch rather than French models, she planned a new Broad Walk paralleling the King's Staterooms, created a bower of elm trees pruned into the form of a living archway, and erected a series of beautiful wrought-iron gates and partitions. The queen also imported many exotic plants from the Americas. While Wren was making Hampton Court more monumental, Mary was restoring her gardens to a more human scale.

At the conclusion of William and Mary's innovations, Hampton Court looked much as it does today. Sadly, however, the finished palace was not to see many more royal festivities on a par with those of the Tudors and early Stuarts. Even before the early death of Mary, William had been forced to move to Kensington Palace in London, where Parliament could keep a closer watch on him, but he still returned to Hampton Court to hunt. When on one of these visits he was thrown from his horse and killed, the Jacobites drank toasts to the mole, "the gentleman in brown velvet," who was given credit for causing the accident.

and his beds of herbs and vegetables. Henry, a fanatical hunter, concentrated on buying up adjacent estates to add to Hampton Court's rural enclosure. Both he and his daughter Elizabeth, who was said to work in her gardens for an hour each morning, designed several charming enclaves featuring native English flowers. Charles II, who had been brought up on the Continent, aspired to relandscape Hampton Court according to the most up-to-date French models. To the east of the palace, he created an entirely new formal garden, featuring parterres, broad open expanses, and straight rows of lime trees, all based on drawings sent from Paris by Louis XIV's gardener Le Nôtre.

This French influence was continued in the reign of James II's daughter Mary and her husband William of Orange. William and Mary were determined to live in high style. In their era this was synonymous with the Baroque magnificence of Louis XIV's palace at Versailles: The Tudor gables, mullioned windows, and irregularly shaped rooms of Hampton Court were dismissed as hopelessly passé. Encouraged by the royal architect, Sir Christopher Wren, they proposed to demolish Hampton Court and rebuild it as an English Versailles.

The southern and easternmost quarters of the old palace were reduced to rubble, and two new wings of state apartments were constructed in their place. The new King's and Queen's Staterooms, with their high ceilings and formal, repetitive façades, could not have been a more jarring contrast to the remaining Tudor courtyards. But Wren's use of red brick and two kinds of white stone provided a semblance of continuity between old and new. Other characteristics, such as the simple repetition of elements and the generous use of glass, suggest a Dutch influence, perhaps first imported by Charles II and later reinforced by William and Mary. Wren's long, light-filled galleries are also magnificent, providing a superior setting for the palace's works of art. Visitors come to the Cartoon, or King's, Gallery to admire the seventeenth-century tapestries based on designs by Raphael; they visit

Right, detail from a fresco by Antonio Verrio depicting Cupid with the British fleet in the background, from a painting dedicated to Queen Anne's husband, George of Denmark. Below, the Goddess of Plenty. Below right, Henry VIII and the Barber-Surgeons, begun by Hans Holbein.

Mary's younger sister Anne assumed the throne. Anne was a sympathetic figure but not an attractive one. Her chief interests were hunting, which she pursued from a one-horse chaise, and eating. She suffered from a combination of obesity, dropsy, and gout and bore thirteen children, none of whom survived to adulthood. When she died in 1714, her coffin was described as "nearly square." Poor Anne had inherited the debts of her brother-in-law, who had treated her shabbily during his lifetime. The muralist Antonio Verrio, hoping to recover some of the money owed to him for his work on Wren's new wings at Hampton Court, returned to the palace and painted a ceiling that depicted Queen Anne as the personification of Justice. This not-so-subtle hint did Verrio little good, however, for he died unpaid.

Upon Anne's death, the crown passed to George of Hanover. This German-born king spent a great deal of time at Hampton Court, but he had little interest in social life and less in palace architecture. After the reign of his son George II, the last noteworthy host at the palace, the English royal households never again took up residence at Hampton Court.

Though much less well recorded than the official chronicles of its royal residents, Hampton Court had always sustained a colony of secret inhabitants. As early as King Henry VIII's time, there were squatters living in some of Cardinal Wolsey's 280 guest bedrooms. (Even though the sovereign might have seen fit to leave a magnificent palace standing empty for months at a time, his stewards were apparently far too sensible to let such fine quarters go to waste.) After a number of rulers had unsuccessfully tried to rid the palace of its illegal residents, George III finally regularized the situation by allowing certain individuals, mostly people of high birth but small means, to live at Hampton Court under the "grace and favor" of the Crown. This tradition continues to this day.

By the early eighteenth century, the trappings of England's royalty were beginning to lose a good deal of their mystery. During the reign of Queen Anne, Hampton Court won its place in English literature. In the course of a card party given by a palace official, one of the gentlemen impetuously snipped a lock of hair from the coiffure of a lady named Arabella Fermor. The silly brouhaha that followed became the talk of London and inspired Alexander Pope's *Rape of the Lock*. In this mock epic Pope waspishly characterizes Hampton Court as the place where "Britain's statesmen oft the fall foredoom/Of tyrants and of nymphs at home" and where "thou, great *Anna*! whom three realms obey,/Dost sometimes counsel take—and sometimes tea."

Built for a commoner with the tastes of a potentate, Hampton Court had by Pope's day become the retreat of a distinctly bourgeois queen. A century later, Queen Victoria would complete the cycle when, over the furious protest of many Tories, she opened the palace and its gardens to the people of London. For the first time in 300 years, even the most lowly could enjoy the sumptuous country estate of a butcher's son.

Below, an engraving (1827) of the Tudor Gatehouse. Ten years later Queen Victoria opened Hampton Court to the public.

Petrodvorets

U.S.S.R.

Peter the Great, czar of Russia from 1682 to 1725, instigated many state and social reforms and opened his backward country to European influences. In his desire for a "window on Europe," he constructed the beautiful Western-style city of St. Petersburg—now Leningrad—on the Gulf of Finland. Nearby he built Peterhof, now Petrodvorets, the most lavish of his summer palaces. Begun by Jean-Baptiste le Blond, it was greatly expanded by the Italian architect Bartolomeo Rastrelli during the reign of Peter's daughter, the Empress Elizabeth I. Preceding page, the northern façade of Petrodvorets, with its famous cascade.

Left, the Neptune fountain (ca. 1650) by the German artists Ritter and Schwider. It was purchased from the city of Nuremberg by Czar Paul I to grace the southern façade of the palace.

Right and below left, the northern façade and the Great Cascade. The water drains into the large central pool containing the Samson fountain. From there it flows through the 500-yard-long Morskoi Canal (below) and empties into the Gulf of Finland. Russian hegemony over the gulf was demonstrated by the settlement of nearby St. Petersburg.

Symbolizing Russia triumphant, a gilded bronze statue of Samson slaying the lion (above left) stands at the heart of the lower park of Petrodvorets. The wooden statue was carved in 1734 in commemoration of the twenty-fifth anniversary of Peter I's victory over Sweden at Poltava. The original was replaced in 1802 with a bronze copy by M. J. Kozlovski. This in turn was destroyed during the siege of Leningrad when Nazi soldiers burned the main palace. The present statue, like the palace itself, is the product of a meticulous, postwar reconstruction of the estate.

An avid student of Western technology, Peter the Great personally worked on the plans for the system of 129 fountains at Petrodvorets. The lasting cultural impact of Peter's visits to Europe can be seen in the mythological theme of the fountain statuary, most of which dates from the late eighteenth century.

Above right, a group of playful mermaids and dolphins at the base of the Great Cascade. The nymph Galatea (below near right), associated with calm waters, is an allusion to Russia's newly won control of the Baltic. Below far right, Psyche, cast from an original by Canova. The statue presides over the gardens of the Monplaisir Pavilion, Peter's favorite residence, where he and his queen, Catherine, were living at the time of his death in 1725.

Below left, left to right: Perseus holding up the head of the Gorgon; Pandora; and a Danaid. The Danaides were the daughters of Danaus who, at their father's behest, murdered their husbands on their wedding nights and were condemned to pour water eternally into a bottomless vessel.

Above, the formal gardens to the west of the Great Cascade. They were restored in 1953 on the basis of an old etching. Below left, the Hermitage, an unpretentious pavilion in the Dutch style where the Empress Elizabeth often entertained her guests with meals she had cooked herself in the tiled kitchen. An oval dining table that could be lowered mechanically into the servants' quarters below protected the privacy of the royalty and their guests. Below right, one of the small summer pavilions in the gardens. Right, less formal fountains. The Pyramid fountain (above far right) is the oldest at Petrodvorets.

Far left, top to bottom, some of the splendidly restored rooms of the main palace: the Throne Hall, also called the Peter Room; the Partridge Room, named for its wallpaper design; and one of the Chinese Rooms, furnished with eighteenth-century European chinoiserie.

The portrait gallery (near left) contains 328 paintings of young women from all over Russia. They were commissioned by Catherine II and executed by Count Pietro Rotari. The Hall of Honor (above) was also redecorated during Catherine's reign; its paintings commemorate the naval battle of Tschemsa. Below, the early nineteenth-century White Room, famous for its five, rock crystal chandeliers.

Following page, Petrodvorets approached along the sea canal. Once the summer playground of the court, the palace is now a people's park.

Petrodvorets U.S.S.R.

By European standards, the Russia into which Peter the Great was born was backward indeed. Muscovy was ruled from the onion-domed towers of the Kremlin, which regarded any idea that smacked of European culture as "against God's will." The wearing of "German" clothes (meaning trousers) was forbidden by law, and Russian brides received three sound lashes with a bullwhip as a traditional part of the wedding ceremony.

The young Peter Romanov seemed an unlikely candidate to change any of this. At seventeen, he was already a giant, six feet eight inches tall, and immensely strong. Peter seized power from his sister with the help of an anti-Western faction of nobles, and then proceeded to devote himself to five years of hard drinking and carousing. His major interest in life was playing practical jokes. Peter organized the revels of an "All Drunken Synod,"

which held orgies under the supervision of a mock patriarch, and he arranged parades of dwarfs and marriages between male courtiers.

Boredom, it is said, began to draw the young czar more and more frequently into Moscow's foreign quarter. These wanderings sparked Peter's interest in European traditions. Then, in 1697, Peter decided that in order to build a strong Russian navy he should visit Europe to study shipbuilding. Although he wished to travel incognito, Peter's gargantuan physique and escort of 125 retainers somewhat inhibited his success. When he appeared at diplomatic functions on the Continent, he often impressed his hosts by his remarkable intelligence and enthusiasm. On other occasions, he made himself equally unforgettable by arriving dressed as a common sailor and belching in the faces of foreign

ambassadors. Peter's notoriously bad manners frequently bordered on psychopathic behavior. While touring a dissecting room in Europe, for example, he forced his companions to take bites out of a defenseless corpse.

Yet this was the same man who vowed to introduce Muscovy to the polite arts. Peter returned from his stay abroad determined to stage a one-man Renaissance. On his homecoming, the czar greeted his boyars (nobles) by whipping out a pair of scissors and cutting off their beards. He personally revised the Russian alphabet and gave demonstrations of scientific dentistry. He outlawed forced marriages. But above all, it was Peter's decision to give Russia its first European-style city—St. Petersburg—that sealed his place in history as a cultural revolutionary. The nineteenth-century Russian poet, Pushkin,

Near right, Peter the Great. Far right, Bartolomeo Rastrelli, the Italian inventor of Russian Baroque and architect of Petrodvorets from 1741 to 1752. Below, the Neva River, where Peter established the fortress of Kronstadt and, later, his new capital of St. Petersburg.

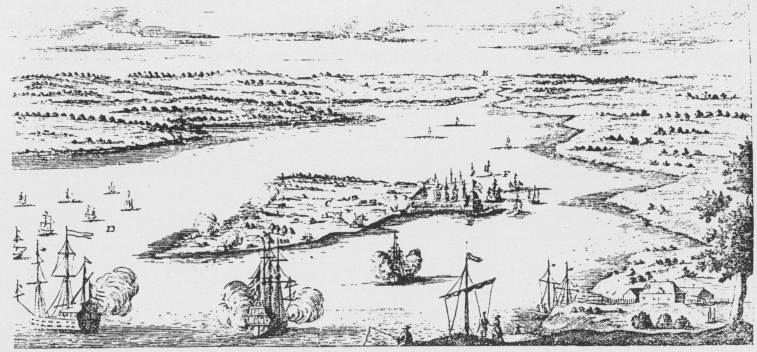

Far left, an equestrian portrait of Catherine II, "the Great." During the reign of this German-born czarina, Yuri Velton, a pupil of Rastrelli, redecorated the rooms of Petrodvorets's main palace in the Neoclassical style which remains today. Even before the death of her husband, Czar Peter III, Catherine entertained her lovers at Monplaisir: Prince Potëmkin (above near left) and Prince Orlov (below near left) were among her numerous favorites.

who loved liberty and hated chauvinism, celebrated Peter as a man of "lofty visions." In Pushkin's portrayal of the czar in his poem, *The Bronze Horseman,* Peter stares across the lonely expanse of the Neva River at the head of the Gulf of Finland and proclaims: "Nature has destined us to open a window on Europe."

Peter's original motivations for founding St. Petersburg, however, were military rather than cultural. Russia was making a bid to replace Sweden as the major Baltic power—a struggle that would take twenty years—and access to the sea via the Gulf of Finland was crucial. In 1703, Russia defeated a Swedish garrison stationed at the mouth of the Neva, and Peter envisioned this strategic spot as a major trading center, built on the model of Amsterdam. No site could have been less suitable to urban living, European-style or otherwise. To make the czar's dream a reality, thousands of serfs labored to drain the swampland. The boyars were then forced to build townhouses there at their own expense. In 1712, the very reluctant royal court packed up and followed the czar from Moscow to St. Petersburg.

As early as 1705, Peter had begun drawing up plans for a lavish summer palace to be situated outside his new capital on the shores of the Gulf of Finland. Two obstacles stood in the way of his project. First of all, the czar had no intention of sharing this home with Eudoxia, his well-bred but insipid queen. Peter was living with Catherine, a former Lithuanian peasant who was much more his equal in brains and drinking ability. In 1707, however, the czar merely decided to ignore Eudoxia's existence and entered into a bigamous marriage with Catherine.

Sweden, a tougher adversary than Eudoxia, was not so easily ignored. The Great Northern War, raging over Swedish supremacy of the Baltic, was not officially over until 1721, even though a decisive battle at Poltava in the Ukraine on July 8, 1709, had turned the tide conclusively in Russia's favor. The Russian Samson, it was said, had gloriously defeated the Swedish lion.

In the wake of this victory, the royal Samson turned to domestic concerns.

Work on the summer palace, which was given the German name of Peterhof, began in 1710. Teams of serfs under the direction of Nicholas Michetti drained the marshes and terraced the slopes which would lead from the palace to the shore. Then they laid the foundation for a vast network of fountains, installing a system of wood-encased lead pipes and digging a 500-yard-long canal, the Morskoi, which would carry the water into the gulf.

Peter's admiration for the Germans and the Dutch was gradually giving way to a fascination for the French. In 1716, the work of designing the palace and gardens was turned over to the architect Jean-Baptiste le Blond, and a year later Peter decided to pay a visit to Louis XV. On this journey, the czar's less than impeccable manners appear to have been under control, and in fact, the French court found him delightful. When Peter left Paris on June 30, 1717, he took with him more than one hundred French artisans and technicians and boundless enthusiasm for the elegant formal gardens of Versailles.

Peter did not really intend to turn his own life into one long public ceremony as the Sun King had done, however. He never even took up residence in the Bolshoi Palaty, or main palace, of Peterhof, as he and Catherine preferred the small, unpretentious pavilions like his favorite, Monplaisir, that dotted the estate grounds. The czar enjoyed supervising the work of the Peterhof gardeners and designing fountains which played elaborate, practical jokes. There were benches that spurted water when sat on by unsuspecting strollers, a realistic tree whose metal leaves suddenly sprayed out jets of water, and countless other trick fountains controlled by operators hidden in the shrubbery. But in 1725, before Peterhof was finished, Peter the Great died, leaving the palace and his throne available to the most powerful bidder.

Although Peter is known to history as "the Great," his death was not especially mourned by his contemporaries. In pursuing his many autocratic reforms, he had bullied the nobility, ignored the suffering of the peasants, and tortured to death his own son and heir, the gentle Alexei. After Peter, the throne passed to a series of weak rulers, most of whom shared his taste for debauchery but lacked his organizational genius. Finally, in 1741, the nobility in desperation deposed the then-reigning czar in favor of Peter's daughter Elizabeth.

The "merry Czarina," as she soon came to be called, shared in the family predilection for sexual escapades. Elizabeth, however, had style. She owned a wardrobe of 15,000 dresses and took the most handsome guardsmen as lovers. For the first time, flagrant drunkenness was discouraged at court, and Russian social life acquired a semblance of sophistication. Soon after ascending the throne, Elizabeth hired the Italian architect Bartolomeo Rastrelli to make Peterhof worthy of her sparkling court.

Rastrelli was the supreme exponent of the Russian Rococo style. At Peterhof, he was restricted to adapting and completing the more Classical designs of le Blond, but he made sweeping changes nonetheless. Between 1747 and 1751, he added a third story to the main palace and doubled the length of the façade by constructing two new wings which ended in elaborate, freestanding pavilions. The palace interior was completely redecorated, with the exception of Peter's personal study. And sections of the gardens were relandscaped in the less formal English manner.

Thus refurbished, Peterhof became a favorite summer playground for the Russian court. Monplaisir was the spot chosen by the future Czarina Catherine the Great and her husband Paul to fight boredom by entertaining their lovers *à quatre*. Later Romanovs enjoyed the sparkling foun-

tains so much that they added to the waterworks, purchasing the celebrated Neptune fountain from the city of Nuremberg and creating the Samson fountain to commemorate Peter's victory at Poltava. Here the biblical giant is depicted forcing open the jaws of the lion.

Against this elegant background, the aristocracy played out a charade born of Peter's ambitious but inherently limited reforms. The courtiers slavishly followed French etiquette, donning their summer

This engraving by Pietro Novelli (above) shows Peter the Great supervising the construction of his new capital of St. Petersburg in 1703.

Below, the palace built by Jean-Baptiste le Blond for Peter. Rastrelli later added another story and doubled the length of the façade.

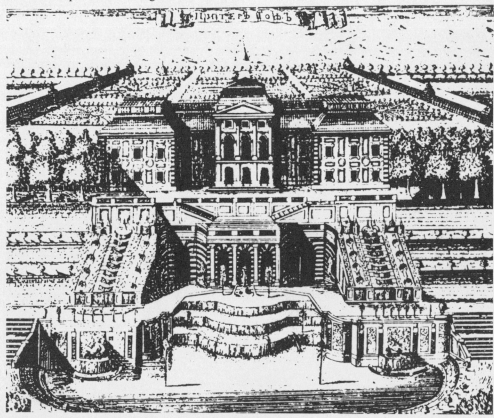

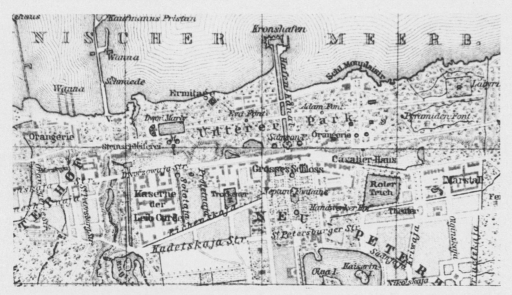

Above, a late nineteenth-century plan of Petrodvorets. It is labeled in German, a language which, along with French, was more widely spoken than Russian at court. The siege of Leningrad, which lasted from August 1941 to January 1944, left Petrodvorets devastated (left). Below, Russian cavalrymen before the gutted palace and denuded cascade.

tury, many of them could not even speak fluent Russian. While Russian agriculture became hopelessly inefficient, the upper classes spent much of their lives peering enviously through Peter's "window on Europe."

Then came the Revolution. But Peterhof, the symbol of Russia's old order, survived. Of all the czars, Peter the Great, with his affinity for progressive European ideas, was one of the few whom the Bolsheviks found sympathetic. Peterhof, its name Russianized to Petrodvorets, became a people's park.

Ironically, it was Europeans who nearly destroyed Peter's monument. In August of 1941, Nazi troops preparing to besiege St. Petersburg—by now called Leningrad—pitched their tents on the grounds of Petrodvorets. The Russians had already removed or buried much of the estate's valuable furnishings and statuary. The Germans cut down trees hundreds of years old for firewood, burnt the Bolshoi Palaty to the ground, and razed the beautiful pavilions, including Monplaisir.

clothes at Easter in spite of the chill northern climate. They flirted with the ideas of the Enlightenment, although many of them privately agreed with the opinion of Czarina Elizabeth, who had pronounced reading bad for the health. Meanwhile, these landowners became less and less aware of what was going on in their own country. By the nineteenth cen-

After the war, restorations of Petrodvorets began immediately, and the grounds were reopened to the public in June 1945. At first the main palace was represented merely by a façade which served as a backdrop for the fountains. But as soon as construction materials and skilled workers became available, it was meticulously reconstructed to the smallest detail. Stalin gave this work top priority. He was in a hurry to erase all memory of the infamous siege of Leningrad. For reasons of his own, he viewed the people's heroic resistance as a threat to his personal legend. While he conducted purges of Leningrad party officials and intellectuals, the people were encouraged to visit Petrodvorets, where they could contemplate the newly gilded Samson fountain. Erected in 1802 to immortalize Peter the Great's victory over the Swedes, the statue had come to serve the purposes of the strongman of another century.

Mirabell Palace

Salzburg, Austria

Mirabell Palace, with its ordered Baroque gardens, is one of the attractions of the Austrian city of Salzburg. The palace was begun in 1606 by the powerful Archbishop Wolfdietrich von Raitenau for his mistress Salome Alt. Today the square, Neoclassical palace built around an inner courtyard serves as municipal offices.

Preceding page, the quiet southern façade, seen beyond the main fountain. The external architecture of the palace is generally restrained, highly regular, and somewhat academic. Contrasting with the nineteenth-century Neoclassicism of the eastern façade (above far left) and the western façade (below left) is the more fanciful, Baroque courtyard façade of the Marmorsaal, or Marble Hall (above near left), the work of Johann Lucas von Hildebrandt.

The two other monuments to episcopal and princely powers are the twin-towered façade of the cathedral and in the background the ancient hilltop citadel of Hohensalzburg (right). The ornamental flower beds of the garden itself were laid out under Archbishop Johann Ernst von Thun in the 1690s.

Below, the main fountain, surrounded by allegorical statues of the four elements by Ottavio Mosto (1690). The elaborate but restrained geometric topiaries are characteristic of Baroque landscape gardening.

Above left, the Mirabell gardens, framed by a side entrance. Below left, the manicured curving patterns of Baroque garden hedges. Below, one of the Classical garden vases designed by Hildebrandt early in the eighteenth century.

The archbishops of Salzburg were great patrons of the secular arts and left a vivid record of their tastes in the many sculptures that adorn the gardens. Far right, top and center, two of Ottavio Mosto's statues of the elements, which stand near the main fountain: Paris Abducting Helen (water) and Hercules Lifting Antaeus (air). Below right, three figures from the Dwarf Garden added by the Archbishop Franz Anton von Harrach in the eighteenth century. Unlike the other statues, Maximilian Röck's 1664 copper figure of Pegasus (above near right) is a recent acquisition, having been moved to the Mirabell grounds in 1913.

The Marmorsaal was the only part of the early eighteenth-century Baroque palace built by Hildebrandt which escaped a city-wide fire in 1818. While much of Mirabell has been converted to offices, the Marmorsaal remains one of the Baroque jewels of Salzburg and today is used as the municipal marriage hall. Above left, the Marmorsaal, with its tall decorative pilasters, rich moldings, and inlaid floors. Below left, two of the gilt medallions which separate the upper and lower areas between the pilasters. The "windows" above them are in fact mirrors.

Above, the eastern end of the Marmorsaal, which projects into the courtyard. Right, the top landing of the Engelstiege (angel staircase)—celebrated for its putti, marble statues, and intricately ornamented balustrade—that leads to the Marmorsaal.

Above center right, the bottom flight of the Engelstiege, with its exuberant balustrade. The staircase (details these pages) was designed by Hildebrandt; the putti (far right) and figures in wall niches (left and immediately above) are the work of Georg Raphael Donner. Center below right, a gilt medallion above the western entrance of the Marmorsaal said to depict Salome Alt, mistress of Archbishop Wolfdietrich von Raitenau (1587–1611). Raitenau built Schloss Altenau—later renamed Schloss Mirabell—for her and their fifteen children. Near right, one of the bronze lamps on the staircase. Top left, some of the gilded decorative stucco work, executed by Carlo Carlone and Gaetano Fanti.

Following page, the courtyard and eastern wing seen from the Marmorsaal. The arched portal leads to the busy Mirabellplatz (Mirabell Square).

Mirabell Palace
Salzburg, Austria

In its various incarnations, Schloss Mirabell, or Mirabell Palace, has been one of the treasures of Salzburg, Austria, since the end of the sixteenth century. The first structure to occupy the site of this dignified Neoclassical building has utterly vanished. Its successor, the beautiful Mirabell of Mozart's day, was nearly destroyed in a city fire more than 150 years ago. The present palace, though not a pure example of any one style of architecture, remains among the most beloved embodiments of the Salzburg spirit.

Today the name Salzburg immediately evokes thoughts of the city's annual music and drama festival and of its most famous son—the composer Mozart. It is the capital of the Austrian province of Salzburg on the border of Bavaria, West Germany—a startlingly beautiful district of placid mountain lakes and changeable mountain weather. Salzburg means "salt city," and the salt trade from the mines of the nearby Salzkammergut gave the province a pivotal position in both Alpine and Bavarian affairs.

For a thousand years, from about the year A.D. 800, the city was the seat of one of the most powerful ecclesiastics of the German-speaking world, the autocratic archbishops of Salzburg. Moreover, from the thirteenth century, the Salzburg archbishops were not only prelates of the see but also secular princes of this wealthy domain, owing only nominal fealty to the Holy Roman Emperor. Thus when Wolfdietrich von Raitenau became archbishop of Salzburg in 1587 at the age of twenty-eight, he inherited a well-established tradition of civic rule by rich and worldly churchmen.

In 1587, the city of Salzburg was little changed from its medieval aspect. It was a cramped but orderly hillside town of steep narrow streets dominated by the imposing bulk of the Hohensalzburg fortress, the great citadel of the medieval archbishops. With a zeal drawn from his own Italian education and part-Medici ancestry, von Raitenau set out to transform Salzburg into a "German Rome." However, as one recent historian remarked, "Salzburg at the end of his reign must indeed have resembled a bombed city." Although von Raitenau lived to finish only one of his projects (fittingly enough, his own mausoleum), Salzburg today bears the indelible imprint of his ambition. A wealth of landmarks which were completed after his death, including many large, open squares and a celebrated Italianate cathedral, illustrates his passion for spacious and monumental effects.

Among von Raitenau's attempts to recreate the ambiance of his Italian upbringing was a resplendent *Lustschloss* (pleasure palace) on the northeast bank of the River Salzach, which was intended to imitate the leisured seclusion of an Italian villa. Here he installed his mistress Salome Alt, daughter of a prosperous Jewish merchant and town councilor.

But the new palace, begun in 1606, was to enjoy only a brief term as Schloss Altenau—named for the rechristened Salome after von Raitenau persuaded Emperor Rudolf II to elevate her and their fifteen children to noble estate. In 1611, von Rai-

Right, an early nineteenth-century engraving by J. A. Corvinus, showing the Mirabell complex before the fire of 1818. The western gardens are at the height of their splendor. Johann Lucas von Hildebrandt's tower can be seen on the eastern façade of the palace.

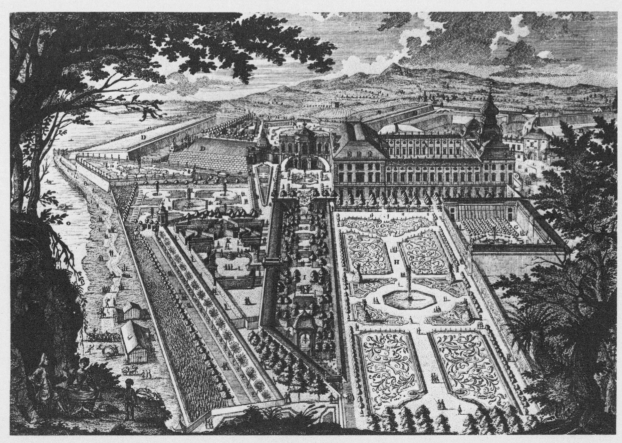

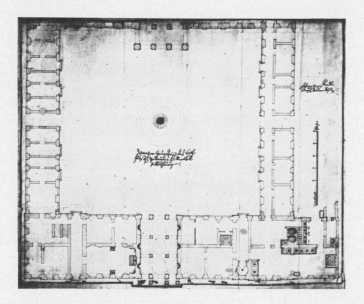

Archbishop Wolfdietrich von Raitenau (above right) built his pleasure palace for his mistress Salome Alt (above center). Above left, a plan of the palace designed by Hildebrandt. Below, a late eighteenth-century drawing of Hildebrandt's eastern façade.

tenau's ill-judged instigation of hostilities against Bavaria caused the cathedral canons to transfer their allegiance to his cousin, Marcus Sitticus von Hohenems. The deposed archbishop was kept prisoner in the Hohensalzburg until his death in 1617. Salome and her children were allowed to escape to the neighboring Austrian province of Carinthia.

Schloss Altenau, renamed Mirabell, began a placid history as a summer palace under the new archbishop Marcus Sitticus (1612–1619) and his successor Paris Lodron (1619–1653). Although no illustrations of the original Mirabell survive, a contemporary account of the "splendid building," with its shining metal-roofed tower and variegated gardens, depicts it as the home of "all sorts of honest delights and diversions." For decades it was substantially unaltered. Paris Lodron, whose term of office coincided with the ravages of the Thirty Years' War (1618–1648), prudently extended the city walls to enclose the Mirabell park. They still form part of the boundaries of the palace's western garden. But it remained for Johann Ernst von Thun, an archbishop with definite architectural opinions, to effect real changes in the grounds themselves.

Von Thun, with his protégé the great architect Johann Fischer von Erlach, transformed Salzburg even more drastically than von Raitenau. Most notably he was responsible for turning large tracts of the Mirabell park into a classic Baroque garden, built on disciplined geometric and spatial effects.

From the south, the view up to the palace façade takes in symmetrical parterres of flowers, bordered on both sides by ornamental stone balustrades with garlanded urns. In the center of the garden is a large octagonal fountain flanked by four statues and conical yew bushes. The statues, the work of the Italian sculptor Ottavio Mosto in 1690, depict mythological events corresponding to the four elements of earth, air, fire, and water. The extravagant motion of the stone figures contrasts remarkably with the geometric and regular arrangement of the live plants.

On the western side of the palace plays a small fountain with a copper statue of Pegasus, thought to be the work of Maximilian Röck (1664). This section, separated from the southern gardens by a wall of shrubbery including a maze—the Irrgarten—and an arcade—the Laubengang—sharply contrasts with the openness and serene geometry of the southern parterres. An oddity here are the stone dwarfs of Archbishop Franz Anton von Harrach (1709–1727). During the Bavarian rule of Salzburg from 1809 to 1815, these twenty-

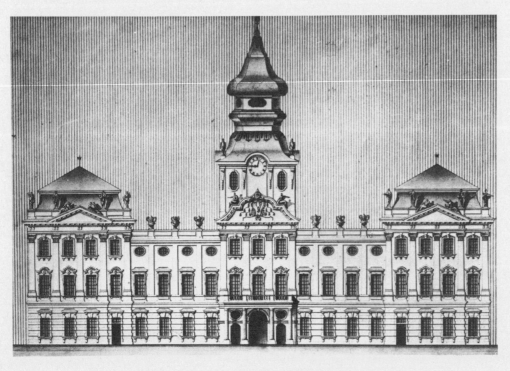

These eighteenth-century engravings by Corvinus of the Mirabell gardens depict: the orangerie (top), the southern parterre (center), and the lower part of the southern parterre (bottom).

eight bizarre little figures so offended the refined sensibilities of Ludwig I that he had them removed from the gardens and sold. Thirteen have since been restored.

The curious mixture of elements in this section is further enriched by a former aviary and an elegant outdoor theater. The aviary dates from about 1700 and is now used to house special exhibits of the city museum. The Heckentheater (hedge theater), composed of topiary shrubbery, is the oldest of its kind in the German-speaking world. Built in 1715, it was once used for operas and concerts.

Along with its gardens, Mirabell Palace was extensively altered in the later Baroque period. However, only a few of these eighteenth-century alterations survive. The Archbishop von Harrach, creator of the dwarf garden, was responsible for the renovations with the help of one of the greatest Austrian architects of the age, Fischer von Erlach's younger rival, Johann Lucas von Hildebrandt. Hildebrandt, however, was obliged to remain in Vienna where he was supervising the construction of the great Belvedere Palace for Prince Eugene of Savoy. Transportation at that time was slow, and weekly lists of questions were prepared in Salzburg and sent to him. By good fortune, his written replies, with plans and drawings, have been preserved. They are the chief remaining evidence of what the entire Mirabell Palace looked like before the terrible fire that swept Salzburg in 1818.

Like the present building, the palace was an enclosed square with a central courtyard. The eastern façade, facing the present Mirabellplatz, was crowned by a lofty central tower and presented an elegantly varied roof line. Unfortunately, nothing remains of Hildebrandt's Mirabell except the spacious Marmorsaal, or Marble Hall, approached by an elaborate staircase.

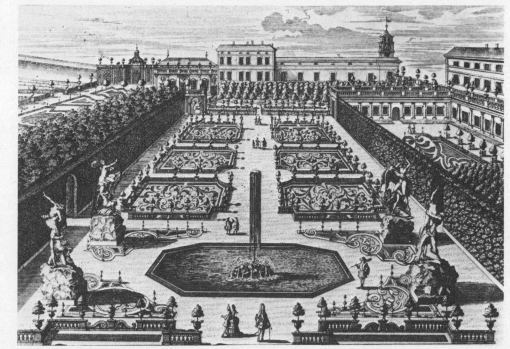

The Marmorsaal remains one of the most striking examples of Baroque interior architecture to be found today. Its eastern end, which projects into the courtyard, is dominated by lofty arched and oval windows that are echoed in the rest of the room by false windows and marble panels. Elaborate gilt stucco work by Jakob Gall adorns the cornices and the capitals of the inlaid marble pilasters. Gilt medallions (including, curiously enough, a portrait said to be of Salome Alt) separate the upper windows from the main windows and corresponding marble panels.

The marble staircase, rising in three flights, boasts a splendid, rhythmic balustrade which is generally regarded as one of the best examples of Hildebrandt's masterful ribbon work. This balustrade is adorned with marble putti by Georg Raphael Donner (1693–1741). The forceful, upward motion in the lines of the staircase is playfully counterpointed by the contortions and pointing fingers of the

irrepressible putti. Today the much-photographed Marmorsaal is often the setting for civil marriage ceremonies performed by the burgomaster of Salzburg.

Hildebrandt's palace remained intact for less than a century. Its best-known tenant during this period was Archbishop Hieronymus Colloredo, remembered primarily for his disdainful treatment of the court organist and assistant conductor, Wolfgang Amadeus Mozart. The archbishop was to receive more than his comeuppance in the Napoleonic Wars, when the principality of Salzburg was stripped of its sovereignty. In the ensuing seesaw realignments of power, Salzburg briefly came under Bavarian rule in 1809, only to be absorbed into the newly created Austrian Empire seven years later.

At the time of the fire of 1818, Mirabell was the property of the Austrian Kaiser Franz I, who called in Peter von Nobile, director of the School of Architecture in Vienna, to rebuild the palace. Von No-

bile's Mirabell stands today as it was built. In contrast to the Baroque palace gardens and the Marmorsaal, it is a sober Neoclassical structure with a nearly unbroken horizontal roof line. The current façades present nothing but a severe rectilinearity described once, perhaps harshly, as "that legendary penny-saving art of good Kaiser Franz."

In the mid-nineteenth century, Franz's great-nephew, Kaiser Franz Joseph, relinquished Mirabell and its gardens to the municipal government of Salzburg. Though let as private apartments for more than half a century, Mirabell has been continuously occupied by the city government since 1938. Today, partitioned and subpartitioned into city offices, much of the interior is barely recognizable as the remnants of a palace. But the grounds have kept much of their former beauty, and the Marmorsaal remains one of the jewels of the Austrian Baroque.

It is doubtful whether Salzburg, the birthplace of Mozart, would be as highly regarded by music lovers today if it weren't for the special Baroque quality of the city and its architecture. And nothing better embodies the spirit of serene and civilized Salzburg than the Mirabell Palace and park—a cheerful convergence of bridal parties, everyday city business, and memories of dignified Classicism and Baroque energy.

Below, a detail from the partial interior elevation of a room (right) sent by Hildebrandt to the builders at Mirabell. Below right, the western courtyard façade. Behind the center is the Marmorsaal, the famed marble hall.

Palace of Sanssouci

Potsdam, East Germany

For forty years, Frederick the Great, king of Prussia, spent as much time as he could at Sanssouci, his summer residence in Potsdam. Built from 1745 to 1747, the 300-foot-long pleasure palace (preceding page) gently crowns a six-tiered, terraced arc of greenhouses.

The outstretched arms of an imposing semicircular colonnade (above, mirrored in rainwater) marks the entrance to Sanssouci. During the summers, Frederick the Great had laurel trees placed between the columns. Ornate vases atop the simple attic balustrade also lighten the formal Classicism of the stately, paired Corinthian columns. Today a simple footpath (below right) leads from the north toward the gates between the break in the colonnade that originally defined the main entrance. A less dramatic approach road (above right) also parallels the main façade. Visible from the entrance colonnade, on top of a nearby hill to the north, are the picturesque sham ruins (left) that disguise the pumps and reservoirs used to supply the ponds and fountains on the grounds of Sanssouci.

Projecting from the center of the south-facing garden façade, which houses the most important rooms at Sanssouci, is the oval Marble Hall (left). The northern entrance colonnade is faintly echoed in the paired pilasters and vase-topped balustrades, but for the most part frivolity replaces formality. The heavy entablature is supported by smiling satyrs and bacchantes—indifferent to the weight they bear—wound with garlands of roses and bunches of grapes (right). Wide terraces and flights of steps cascade down the low hill before the south façade (above). Each tier of the terrace holds grapevines and flowers sheltered behind glass. Yew trees shaped into obelisks alternate with dwarf fruit trees in front of the greenhouse. Flanking the bottom flight are statues of Venus and Mercury by Jean Baptiste Pigalle, presented to Frederick by Louis XV of France.

Frederick chose the French name—meaning "without care"—for his pleasure palace and had it inscribed in large bronze letters on the entablature of the Marble Hall (left). In the eighteenth century, French was the universal language of culture and diplomacy and was the language used at Frederick's court.

The domed roof of the hall above the inscription is enlivened by Rococo urns and dormer windows straddled by childlike putti. The top consists of an oculus and a simple, low railing.

This intricate ironwork pavilion (above right) is one of a pair located on the top terrace and linked to the palace by an ironwork trellis with large circular openings. Like the domed roof over the Marble Hall, its "roof" is crowned with a simple, circular railing surrounding an open oculus. The paired Corinthian pilasters with their gilded capitals again recall the entrance portico of the palace. A spectacular gilded sunburst over the entrance to the pavilion reminds visitors that the roots of the elegance of Sanssouci are found in the French court of the Sun King, Louis XIV.

Outbuildings, such as those near the Fountain Pool and canal (below near right), were added to the palace grounds as Sanssouci grew in importance. Today, tourists are free to stroll through these grounds, once reserved for kings and courtiers (below far right).

Sunlight plays on the shallow fountain basin and the thousands of panes of glass of the greenhouses at Sanssouci (near left and bottom far left). The low and graceful palace gates (center far left) lead to long avenues shaded by trees (top far left). And amid the shaped shrubs and trees stand large Baroque statues of Classical figures caught in dynamic poses.

Earth (above) is one of four statues by the French sculptor L. S. Adam given to Frederick by Louis XV. The French king's gifts to the Prussian monarch were diplomatic courtesies; Louis thought little of Frederick, disdainfully calling him "le Marquis de Brandenbourg" rather than "le Roi de Prusse."

Sphinxes with realistic female features (above far left) were common ornaments in Baroque gardens like the one at Sanssouci. Frederick's brother Prince Henry had in his garden two such statues, which reputedly resembled Madame de Pompadour and the Empress Maria Theresa—both enemies of Prussia. Above near left, the "Naughty Children" railing which stands before the lawn of the Picture Gallery.

Below left, a sculptural group added to Sanssouci's garden long after Frederick's reign. It reflects Neoclassical sobriety rather than the frivolity and dynamism of the earlier Rococo and Baroque ornaments. Right, Sanssouci landscaping typical of the nineteenth-century preference for more "natural" gardens. Even here, however, the shape of the canal and the positioning of the trees were carefully planned.

Below, F. G. Adam's Cleopatra Mourned by Amor, *seen through the circular opening of the west iron trellis on the top terrace. The busts of Roman emperors are eighteenth-century reproductions.*

In Sanssouci's gardens the original French formality has largely been replaced by an English naturalness, typified by the canal that meanders throughout the park (above left). Beyond the canal is the Chinese Pavilion (below left), the most fantastic outbuilding of the palace. Designed by Johann Gottfried Büring, with chinoiserie statues by Johann Peter Benkert and Johann Gottlieb Heymüller, it was barely completed before Frederick led his troops into the Seven Years' War in 1756.

Sanssouci was too small for Frederick the Great's paintings and sculptures, so he built a separate building, the Picture Gallery, in the palace grounds (above and right). The building was constructed between 1755 and 1760 by Johann Büring, who had replaced Georg Wenzeslaus von Knobelsdorff as Frederick's principal architect. Like the palace, the single-story Picture Gallery is set close to the ground and consists of two long wings flanking a central oval vestibule. But the dome of this pavilion has all the grand touches the king denied to the crown of the palace. The tall cupola is mounted by a gold Prussian eagle and encircled by large allegorical figures and putti. The statuary below is somewhat more restrained than the Rococo figures on the garden façade of the palace.

Frederick's Picture Gallery consists of one long room, interrupted at the center by the entrance vestibule. The entrance side has large windows that let in natural light for viewing the paintings on the opposite, windowless wall. The ornamentation of the gallery is rich but restrained so that attention is not drawn away from the paintings. The slightly vaulted ceiling is decorated with gilded stucco reliefs of artists' accouterments along with baskets and vines that playfully suggest an outdoor painting expedition. Once again, paired Corinthian columns in the center and at the ends of the gallery recall the entrance portico of the palace. The hall contains a handsome collection of Neoclassical statues and busts including Diana the Huntress (immediately above). Today many of the pieces in the gallery are copies of those Frederick obtained by purchasing the collection of antiquities owned by Cardinal de Polignac in Rome. The originals are now in the Berlin Museum.

The focal point of the interior of Sanssouci is the elliptical Marble Hall (left and right), whose windowed side forms the curved wall at the center of the garden façade. Of all the rooms in the palace, this hall most fully realizes the original vision of the architect, Georg Wenzeslaus von Knobelsdorff. Here, again, paired Corinthian columns are used. The gilded stucco ceiling decorations have a martial theme, and the allegorical figures resting on the cornice represent the arts, thus reflecting two sides of Frederick's character. The chandeliers are of French rock crystal in silver settings, and the walls are faced in marble.

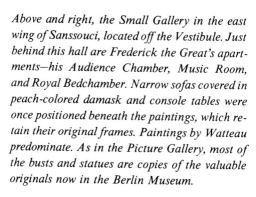

Above and right, the Small Gallery in the east wing of Sanssouci, located off the Vestibule. Just behind this hall are Frederick the Great's apartments—his Audience Chamber, Music Room, and Royal Bedchamber. Narrow sofas covered in peach-colored damask and console tables were once positioned beneath the paintings, which retain their original frames. Paintings by Watteau predominate. As in the Picture Gallery, most of the busts and statues are copies of the valuable originals now in the Berlin Museum.

Above left, the Vestibule of the palace and the entrance to the Small Gallery. The ceiling painting, Flora with Genii, is by Johann Harper; the seated statue of Mars is by L. S. Adam.

The columns in the Marble Hall (above right) are made of white marble veined with gray; their bases and capitals are gilded bronze. The Neo-classical statue by F. G. Adam is of Venus, the goddess of love. Below left, the inlaid marble floor of the hall. Below right, the Small Gallery, reflected in one of its large mirrors framed by golden grapevines.

Right, the Royal Bedchamber. Shortly after Frederick the Great died in this room, his nephew and heir, Frederick William II, had the room redecorated in the Neoclassical style. Its correct Classical proportions contrast with the inventive Rococo style of the Music Room, seen through the door on the left.

Nearly every evening he was in residence, Frederick staged a concert in his Music Room (below left and above near left). He usually played the flute (preserved in the glass case on the pianoforte) accompanied by his court musician Karl Philipp Emanuel Bach. Above far left, a stucco relief panel, The Triumph of Bacchus, above the door between the Marble Hall and the Vestibule. The gilded panel celebrates the vineyard setting of Sanssouci.

Above and top right, the Blue and White Guest Room. Bottom right, the Red and White Guest Room.

Center right, the alcove in the Royal Bedchamber. The Ionic columns, added by Frederick William III, are distinctly out of character with the paired Corinthian columns so prominent throughout the palace and its outbuildings.

Palace of Sanssouci Potsdam, East Germany

It can be a fascinating—if ultimately useless—pastime to re-create the course of history as it might have been without the presence of even just one of its major protagonists. The exercise is particularly interesting if the figure played a dominant role in history against considerable odds. It is easily argued, for example, that the childhood of Frederick the Great of Prussia would have better prepared him for early madness than historical greatness.

Frederick was not the first but the third heir-presumptive of that name born to the then Crown Prince Frederick William of Prussia and his consort Sophia Dorothea. The first Frederick died at his christening when the weight of the little crown placed on his head supposedly crushed his skull. The second Frederick's life was even shorter. He was reputedly frightened to death by the cannons fired to announce his birth. But the third Frederick, born on January 24, 1712, when Prussia had been a kingdom for a mere eleven years, was to live to the age of seventy-four and develop his provincial kingdom into a great European power.

This Frederick's grandfather—Frederick I, who died when the prince was a year old—had built lavish palaces and lived in the grand style of France's Louis XIV. When Frederick's father succeeded to the throne as Frederick William I, he was determined to restore Prussia's fiscal soundness and to strengthen its weak army. "I am the King of Prussia's Finance Minister and his Field Marshal," he declared, and he did indeed put the young country back in order. But Frederick William I soon began showing signs of madness—distrust of others, uncontrollable rages, and strange obsessions. Today, it is known that he suffered from porphyria, the same metabolic malady to affect his relative George III of Britain.

Frederick William had definite ideas about the education of his heir and put him through army drills and Lutheran catechism classes. He would not allow the prince to study the classics, ancient history, poetry, or music. When he caught Frederick's tutor teaching his son Latin, he became so enraged he beat both the prince and the tutor. In defiance of the restrictions on music, the prince held secret concerts in his chambers, with lookouts on guard for his father. If the king approached, the musicians were under instructions to hide themselves in the closets.

As the king's illness worsened, his attacks against his son became even more violent. He lashed out at him with his cane, dragged him around by the hair, and

Below, a 1765 engraving of the southern garden side of Sanssouci. The six terraces that gradually descend from the palace were created to adapt to the terrain upon which Frederick the Great's hermitage was built. Over the years, all of the surrounding gardens underwent far more extensive changes than did the terraces and palace.

Frederick the Great of Prussia (above) well deserved his pleasure palace. His childhood was unhappy, his marriage undesired, and nearly a third of his reign (1740–1786) was occupied in fighting wars.

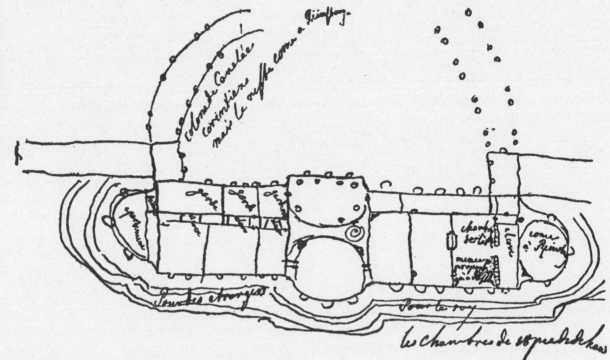

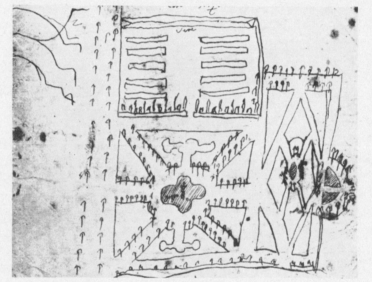

Above and left, two rough drawings that Frederick the Great made in 1744 for his proposed palace and part of its gardens. As can be seen, he had already decided on a Corinthian colonnade, two wings flanking a central pavilion—one for guests (Pour les étrangers) *and the other for himself* (Pour le roi)—*as well as the terraced hill before the southern façade.*

throttled him vigorously. In response to his father's behavior, Frederick developed a calm, icy detachment toward the king, even daring to taunt him. Frederick's love of music, art, and French literature grew in direct proportion to his father's loathing of them. The prince scoffed at the king's strict Protestantism, declaring himself to be a freethinker. He despised hunting, beer drinking, and smoking, his father's greatest pleasures.

Finally, at age eighteen, Frederick decided he could no longer endure the king's abuse. While on a diplomatic tour through Germany with his father, he planned to flee, first to France, then England. But Frederick was caught and imprisoned in the fortress at Küstrin, where by order of his father he would have been forced to witness the beheading of his accomplice, Hans Hermann von Katte—had Frederick not fainted at the last moment. The king had Frederick brought before a military court, and only the intercession of other German rulers persuaded him to spare his son's life. After being released from prison, Frederick was compelled to serve in the regiment at Küstrin, where he lived on a meager allowance and was very closely watched.

Frederick realized that the only escape from virtual imprisonment in a garrison town or a life of fear at his father's court would be to marry and to establish his own

residence. So when his father demanded he marry Elisabeth Christine of Brunswick, Frederick surprised the king by acquiescing. The marriage occurred in June 1733. The prince, however, did not hide his true feelings. He wrote: "I will keep my word and marry the lady; but then it will be *bonjour, Madame, et bon chemin"* (good day, Madame, and good luck on your way).

The young couple were given the palace of Schönhausen near Berlin. But even this was too close for Frederick and for his father. The prince was posted to the regiment at Ruppin and presented with an old manor house nearby at Rheinsberg. Among his fellow officers at Ruppin was Georg Wenzeslaus von Knobelsdorff, an

architect whom Frederick commissioned to redesign his house in a lighter, airier style. Frederick's favorite room there came to be the library Knobelsdorff fashioned out of one floor of a round tower. Here Frederick often spent as much as seven hours a day reading and writing.

In 1736, Frederick began corresponding with Voltaire, the contemporary philosopher he most admired. Voltaire helped the prince to perfect his French prose and encouraged him in writing the treatise *Antimachiavel.* This book took issue with Machiavelli, holding that a sovereign ought to be guided by "virtue" and "natural law" and that "the ruler is in no way the absolute lord of the people under him, but merely the first servant of the state."

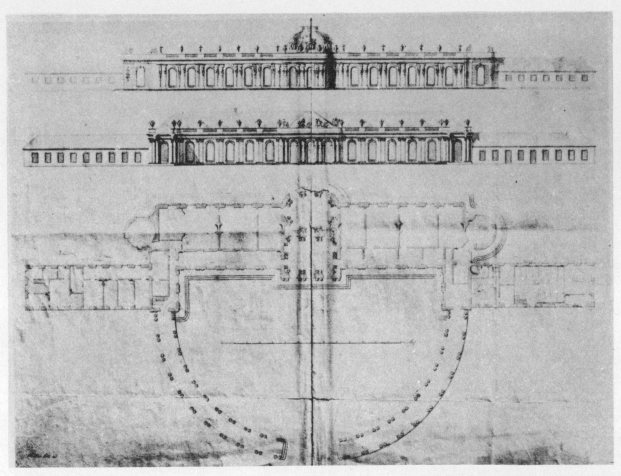

Above, Georg Wenzeslaus von Knobelsdorff (1699–1754), the principal architect of Sanssouci. Knobelsdorff wanted to design a more imposing palace, but the king insisted that his own plan be carried out.

Left, Knobelsdorff's south and north elevations and floor plans.

Such ideas were not so novel as unusual for having been written by a monarch.

On May 31, 1740, Frederick William I died. Having decided against an elaborate coronation, Frederick simply took the oath of office. Then he set in motion the reforms he had dreamed about as crown prince. Voltaire hailed the ascension of the "philosopher king" and addressed him as "Your Humanity."

As king, Frederick abolished torture as a means of judicial inquiry and retained flogging only for army deserters. He limited the death penalty to serious crimes and allowed it only with his approval. Censorship of books was ended and freedom of the press was granted.

The death of Holy Roman Emperor Charles VII in October 1740 turned Frederick's attention from domestic reform to international affairs. Charles had left only a female heir—Maria Theresa—so the Hapsburg claim to the imperial crown was substantially weakened. While the other rulers of Europe busied themselves with the diplomatic maneuvering and saber rattling that would eventually develop

Right, a sketch from Knobelsdorff's notebook of the pilaster figures on the garden façade.

into the War of the Austrian Succession, Frederick moved swiftly. He invaded and conquered the Austrian province of Silesia (now part of Poland) in a mere seven weeks.

By the end of 1745, Frederick's victories had earned him the appellation "Great," and he felt justified in returning home to concentrate on more peaceful matters. Indeed, he had already begun to turn some of his attention to his private affairs by deciding to separate from his wife and build his own summer palace at Potsdam.

In the autumn of 1744, Frederick ordered that a low, south-facing hill on royal grounds just outside Potsdam be reshaped into a six-tiered terrace and planted with grapevines behind glass. He then pre-

sented a sketch of his proposed palace atop the hill to his friend Knobelsdorff. Unlike his grandfather, Frederick I, who had built palaces to impress the other monarchs of Europe, Frederick II was interested only in building a modest, comfortable retreat for himself. Frederick expressed this intent in the French name he chose for the palace—Sans Souci—meaning "without care." (Over the years, his German subjects and their descendants have insisted on spelling the name as one word.)

Frederick's sketch showed only ten principal rooms. His notes written on the drawing in French indicated that the west wing was for guests and their servants, while the east wing was to house his own

The playful garden façade of Sanssouci (above) contrasts with the more formal entrance façade (left) as depicted in 1770 copperplate engravings. The architect von Knobelsdorff had wanted to raise the garden façade off the ground, but the king insisted that he be able to step directly out of the palace onto a wide terrace.

suite. He requested that his bedroom have the same proportions as his room in the Town Palace of Potsdam, recently remodeled by Knobelsdorff. The adjoining library was to be round, like his library at Rheinsberg. For the entrance façade, he wrote that he wanted a semicircular colonnade with paired Corinthian columns, similar to the one Knobelsdorff had added to the Rheinsberg palace.

Construction of Sanssouci began in early 1745. Each stage of the design and construction, including cost estimates, had to be approved by Frederick. Knobelsdorff was frustrated in his efforts to expand upon the king's modest plan. He wanted to raise the palace to two stories, purportedly to protect it from dampness but also with an ulterior motive to make it more imposing when seen from the bot-

tom of the hill. But Frederick wanted to be able to walk directly out of the house into his garden and, of course, he had his way.

On May 2, 1747, the king moved into the still unfinished palace, holding a banquet and a concert for two hundred people to celebrate the event. The interior was not fully completed until the next year.

The years before the outbreak of the Seven Years' War in 1756 were Frederick's happiest. During this time, Sanssouci was filled with guests—mostly men—interested in literature, philosophy, diplomacy, music, and art. Frederick's colleagues were fluent in French (the only language in which he habitually spoke, wrote, and thought), had a sharp wit, and were willing to bear the brunt of the king's own cutting humor. Foreign diplomats who were also interesting conversational-

ists were especially welcome, as Frederick could then mix business with pleasure.

In Frederick's time the main approach to Sanssouci led up a steep slope to a break in the center of the impressive, semicircular colonnade. When designing this entrance, Knobelsdorff was given the freedom to create the grand imperial setting he felt was appropriate for his king. The paired Corinthian columns found here are repeated in the Vestibule and the Marble Hall just beyond it as well as in the ironwork pavilions and Picture Gallery in the garden.

The Vestibule within the north entrance is the most formal space in the palace. It is a rectangular room that, despite its formality, has touches that hint at the gaiety within. Ornamental woodcarvings on the doors by Johann Christian Hoppenhaupt and gilded stucco relief panels above them by Georg Franz Ebenhech have bacchanalian themes, strengthening the association between the palace and its "vineyard" setting.

Beyond the Vestibule is the elliptical Marble Hall, the heart of Sanssouci. Light floods into the chamber from a skylight above and three tall windows opening onto the terraces to the south. In the early years of Sanssouci, a large, round table was brought into the Marble Hall for dining, and there Frederick presided over the many gatherings of gifted politicians, artists, and musicians.

To the left of the Marble Hall is the Audience Chamber, where Frederick received his visitors. While waiting here for the king, one could step out onto a broad terrace, the top level of the many terraces and flight of stairs that cascade down the hill to a large, square formal garden. (In the nineteenth century, the small basin in the center of the garden was enlarged to form the round fountain pond seen today.) Grapes and other fruits as well as flowers that could not survive northern Germany's harsh climate were sheltered in the southward-facing greenhouses that stretched out along the length of each of the six terrace walls. Many sculptures, including large French Rococo pieces presented to Frederick by Louis XV and antique busts and statues acquired by Fred-

Especially in its early years before the Seven Years' War, Sanssouci was the scene of much convivial entertainment. Dinners (left) were held at a large, round table set up in the Marble Hall and concerts (below) were given in the Music Room. Frederick the Great played the flute for many of these fetes. Women were rarely guests at dinner but were welcomed for the concerts. Frederick's dinners had the reputation of being among the wittiest, most intellectually stimulating gatherings in Europe.

Left, the estate of Sanssouci as it looks today. The original Orangerie (page 97, far left) was converted into reception and guest rooms (Neue Kammern) between 1774 and 1776. The much larger Orangerie shown here was completed in 1857. Frederick commissioned the new winter palace (Neues Palais), although he never lived in it himself. Frederick William IV, king of Prussia from 1840 to 1861, made many changes and additions to the gardens and palace. His queen was the last person to reside at Sanssouci.

erick from the estate of Cardinal de Polignac, decorated the surrounding garden.

Beyond the Audience Chamber is the Music Room where Frederick held concerts almost every evening he was in residence—often including his own compositions, some of which are still performed today. Frederick himself would often play the flute, accompanied on the pianoforte by Karl Philipp Emanuel Bach, one of his court musicians. Karl's father, Johann Sebastian Bach, is said to have been very impressed by Frederick's musical knowledge and abilities.

The decor of the Music Room is especially delicate and beautiful. The walls and ceiling are white with all the embellishments in gold. Tall, ornately framed mirrors alternate with scenes from Ovid's *Metamorphoses* by the court painter Antoine Pesne. The ceiling is a garden fantasy. Intricate latticework is entwined with creeping vines, and cupids try to snare exotic birds or sound horns as hares and small dogs race by. And in the center of the ceiling is a golden spider web.

Beyond the Music Room is the Royal Bedchamber, also used as an office, and beyond that is Frederick's circular library, which no one was allowed to enter without special permission. Along the north side of this wing is the Small Gallery, containing part of the king's extensive collection of paintings and sculptures.

Honored guests stayed in one of the five rooms across the Marble Hall from the king's suite. The most famous of these chambers is the Voltaire Room. If Voltaire ever actually stayed in this room, it was before Frederick had it redecorated. After years of urging by the king, Voltaire finally came to live at Sanssouci in 1750. But the decision proved disappointing for both men. Though they continued to admire each other's intellect, their personalities clashed. Voltaire soon embroiled himself in public scandals, making it necessary for him to move out of Sanssouci to Potsdam. It was then that the king had the guest room redecorated, perhaps in expectation of the writer's return. The refurbished room, never seen by Voltaire, was decorated by Johann Christian Hoppenhaupt with life-size painted bird, monkey, and flower reliefs on highly lacquered walls. The enamel and porcelain Meissen chandelier is in the shape of a basket of hanging flowers.

After moving out of Sanssouci, Voltaire published a cruel satire on Pierre de Maupertuis, the president of the Berlin Academy. Frederick was furious. And then in March 1753, Voltaire left Prussia without the king's permission. Both men had behaved badly; it was some time before they renewed their correspondence. After 1774, the king ordered a bust of Voltaire from the porcelain factory he had established in Berlin and placed it in the Voltaire Room.

In 1756, the near decade of peace Frederick had enjoyed at Sanssouci was shattered by his own precipitation of the Seven Years' War from which he was not to return to Sanssouci until 1763. Empress Maria Theresa of Austria had never forgiven Frederick for seizing Silesia in 1740. She now allied herself with France, Russia, and Sweden against Prussia. Austria wanted Silesia back, Russia coveted East Prussia, and Sweden eyed part of the Baltic province of Pomerania. As the Prussian army was outnumbered twenty to one, Frederick decided that once again he must strike first. While his enemies mobilized for the next spring, in late August he attacked and quickly conquered Saxony. His troops then marched into Bohemia, where they were stopped by the Austrians.

But time and fate were not on his side. By 1758, the Russians had captured all of East Prussia. Three of Frederick's closest friends had been killed in battle. His brother and heir, Augustus William, had died. The greatest blow, however, was the death of his sister Wilhelmina. In that year he wrote: "I, who used to be as frisky as a young horse bounding in a field, have become as slow as old Nestor, greying, eaten with grief, riddled with infirmities, just about fit to be thrown to the dogs."

Berlin and Potsdam were occupied by enemy forces in 1760, but Sanssouci was spared. Prussia's condition looked so bleak in 1761 that Frederick seriously contemplated suicide: "Having sacrificed my youth to my father and my maturity to the state, I believe I have the right to dispose of my old age." But the new year brought with it news of the death of Empress Elizabeth of Russia. Her unbalanced nephew Peter III, a passionate admirer of Frederick, switched sides, aligning his country with Prussia. Sweden, Russia's old enemy, then quit the war in disgust. In February 1763, the last combatants signed a peace treaty returning the map of Europe to its prewar state.

At last, Frederick could return to Sanssouci—where his thoughts had been even while at war. During that time, Frederick had commissioned the Friendship Temple (Freundschaftstempel), a round marble pavilion sheltering a life-size statue of his sister Wilhelmina. This

These three eighteenth-century prints show the diversity of the architecture found in the gardens of Sanssouci. Top, the Picture Gallery, modeled after the long galleries of French Renaissance chateaux. Center, the Chinese Pavilion, an example of Rococo whimsy. Bottom, a romantic garden colonnade on the main walk between Sanssouci's garden and the Neues Palais.

somber memorial contrasted sharply with the giddy Chinese Pavilion that had been finished the year the war started. In 1763, work began on a large winter residence, the Neues Palais, designed by the architect Johann Büring—von Knobelsdorff had since died. Located on the western edge of the park of Sanssouci, Frederick had it built to provide work for the artisans of Berlin and to let the world know that the war had not drained Prussia's treasury. He never lived in the new palace.

Frederick's old vitality had left him. Often ill—suffering from gout and dropsy—he scorned physicians, calling them the "impotent witnesses of our suffering." Weak and toothless, he could no longer play the flute in public. The round dining table was rarely set up in the Marble Hall. He usually dined alone or with a few guests in the Audience Chamber.

The king also became sloppy in his personal habits, always dressing in the same threadbare military coat and worn boots. His subjects immediately recognized the frail, stooped old man when he was out walking or riding in his carriage and affectionately called him "Old Fritz."

Despite his decrepit appearance, Frederick's mind was as quick as ever. He carefully nurtured the pre-eminence in German affairs he had gained for his country. From the first partition of Poland in 1770, he obtained the territory that separated Brandenburg and East Prussia, and from 1778 to 1789, by doing little more than mobilizing his still-powerful army, Frederick convinced Austria not to interfere with the independence of Bavaria.

In the autumn of 1785, Frederick remained at Sanssouci weeks later than was customary. Perhaps he thought that this would be his last season at his beloved summer palace. But he returned again the following spring, urging himself to keep going as long as he could. At Sanssouci on August 17, 1786, Frederick passed away after sustaining a chill during a troop review held in pouring rain.

Frederick the Great's will requested that he be buried in the tomb he had prepared on the top terrace of Sanssouci, near the remains of his favorite horse and dogs.

But his nephew and heir, Frederick William II—a pompous and rather foolish man—thought this to be beneath the great king's dignity. So Frederick was buried in the Garrison Church at Potsdam next to his father, the man from whom Frederick had so desperately tried to escape during his youth.

Within weeks of his uncle's death, Frederick William II began remodeling the Royal Bedchamber at Sanssouci. The lively Rococo embellishments were removed to be replaced by "correct" Neoclassical details. The alcove was framed in Ionic columns, which are discordant with the repeated theme of paired Corinthian columns found elsewhere in the palace and on the grounds. Frederick the Great's furniture, including the simple campaign bed in which he always slept, was given to the caretaker. Fortunately, Frederick William did not "modernize" any of the other rooms of Sanssouci.

Frederick William III (1797–1840) rarely stayed at Sanssouci, preferring another palace at Paretz. In 1806, Napoleon entered Potsdam and took up residence in the Town Palace. Fortunately, he spared all of the nearby royal palaces. Then in 1830, Frederick William III had nearly all the antique busts at Sanssouci transferred to the new Berlin Museum, replacing them with copies.

Alterations made by King Frederick William IV in the 1840s and 1850s showed surprising sensitivity to the original design. He enlarged the palace by raising the side wings to two stories and upgraded the servants' quarters and workrooms to family and guest rooms. Within the principal chambers, he consciously preserved the spirit of Frederick the Great.

Frederick William IV was the only other king of Prussia besides Frederick the Great to die at Sanssouci, succumbing there on January 2, 1861. His wife continued to use the palace until her death in 1873, after which Sanssouci was never again inhabited.

Left, a somewhat romanticized painting of Frederick the Great in his later years looking out over his beloved garden from a window at Sanssouci. He holds one of his flutes which, in his last years, he was unable to play when he lost all his teeth. Though in his youth Frederick had loved silks and bright colors, here he wears the threadbare army coat and boots that became his everyday attire until he died. Because of this, the Prussians dubbed him "Old Fritz."

Spanish Steps

Rome

Preceding page and below, the renowned Spanish Steps, or Scala di Spagna, in Rome. Built by the architect Francesco De Sanctis from 1723 to 1726, the staircase links the Piazza di Spagna below with the church and convent of Trinità dei Monti on the Via Sistina, begun in 1495. At the top of the 132 steps stands a Roman obelisk, erected in 1788, which is an imitation of an Egyptian obelisk dedicated to the pharaohs Seti and Rameses the Great.

Babington's Tea Room (above far left) at 23 Piazza di Spagna was a favorite with British tourists in the eighteenth century and is still a popular rendezvous today.

Left, the Via Condotti, which leads from the Tiber and the Vatican toward the bottom of the steps. This narrow artery (top), seen from the large central landing of the steps, is lined with fashionable shops.

Immediately above, the travertine balustrade rising from the first landing of the steps. Artisans and artists take advantage of the expanse of the central landing to display their work to passers-by (right).

The house on the piazza where John Keats, the English Romantic poet, died on February 24, 1821 (top left) has been made into a museum. Above, one of the travertine pedestals that divide the broad base of the steps. Left and below far left, the balustrade-crowned wall of the central landing.

Ironically, the Spanish Steps were both conceived and endowed by the French. The proposal for their construction was first made in the seventeenth century by Louis XIV's minister Cardinal Mazarin, and they were later subsidized by a legacy from a French diplomat. The name, however, was derived from the Spanish embassy, which moved onto the square when the idea was first under consideration.

Charles Dickens once characterized the Spanish Steps as being thronged with unemployed "artist models" in native costume. Even today the steps are crowded with students, tourists, artists, and musicians from all over the world (above and left). Above left, one of the eight bronze lampposts that still decorate and illuminate the bustling piazza.

The descent from the Trinità dei Monti (above right) consists of seventeen flights of stairs, broken and enlivened by landings and changes of direction. The balustraded landings (below near right) and the expanse of the marble steps (below far right) provide ample opportunity for people-watching and relaxing.

The views on these pages attest to the success of the design of the architect Francesco De Sanctis, who wanted to build the grand staircase as a place "for sitting and resting as well as for wide open spaces for free movement."

Today the past is evoked by Babington's window (below center right) and a horse and buggy with a dozing driver (below far right).

Spanish Steps Rome

In August 1820, the English Romantic poet John Keats wrote to his friend Percy Bysshe Shelley in Rome: "There is no doubt that an English winter would put an end to me and do so in a lingering hateful manner, therefore I must either voyage or journey to Italy as a soldier marches up to a battery." Only six months later, in February 1821, Keats died in Rome. The house where he spent the last days of his life is now a memorial museum to both Shelley and Keats. Its front door opens onto the busy Piazza di Spagna, while the tiny room in which he died looks out on the sunny open spaces of one of the spectacular achievements of Roman Baroque architecture, the Spanish Steps.

The Piazza di Spagna is so named be-cause the Spanish Embassy to the Holy See was established there in the early seventeenth century. The Spanish Steps were built in the eighteenth century, providing a broad passageway to—as well as a grand setting for—the fifteenth-century church of Trinità dei Monti (Trinity of the Mountains), which stands atop a steep hill eighty-four feet above the Piazza di Spagna.

The area of Rome around the Spanish Steps and the Piazza di Spagna is known as the foreign quarter. Keats and Shelley were just two of the hundreds of artists and writers drawn there from all over Europe. People of all nationalities and from all walks of life thronged the piazza and the steps, pausing to chat on the landings or beside the Barcaccia—the fountain of the broken ship—in the piazza. Foreign intellectuals, priests in long robes, students, missionaries, and European emissaries to the Holy See mingled with Romans passing the time of day or going about their daily business.

Many famous foreign visitors took lodgings in the Piazza di Spagna or nearby streets during their stay in Rome, including the Flemish painter Peter Paul Rubens. His later work was said to have been inspired by the famous fresco, *The Deposition,* by Daniele da Volterra in the Trinità dei Monti. There were also musi-cians—Liszt, Wagner, Berlioz, and Mendelssohn—as well as numerous writers and poets—Tennyson, Stendhal, Balzac, Hans Christian Andersen, and Byron—who were at various times habitués of this inspirational quarter of Rome.

Travelers today still see essentially the same Piazza di Spagna that Keats found when he arrived in 1820. For the most part, the foreign quarter took on its present aspect between 1495 and 1726. In the fifteenth century the area was virtually a suburb on the outskirts of the old and established center of Rome. The site of the future Spanish Steps was a steep dirt bank of trees, wildflowers, and medieval houses.

In 1495, Charles VIII of France built the church of Trinità dei Monti at the top of its hill. However, the church was not consecrated until 1585, the year in which Cardinal Felice Peretti became Pope Sixtus V. A remarkable and energetic man, who is sometimes called the father of modern town planning, Sixtus had an enormous and lasting influence on the city of Rome. During the five years of his pon-

Above, Sixtus V, pope from 1585 to 1590. His ideas of urban organization transformed Rome and laid the foundation of modern town planning. Left, a seventeenth-century engraving of Trinità dei Monti. The church, begun in 1495, was linked to the Piazza di Spagna by a dirt road until the Spanish Steps were constructed (1723–1724).

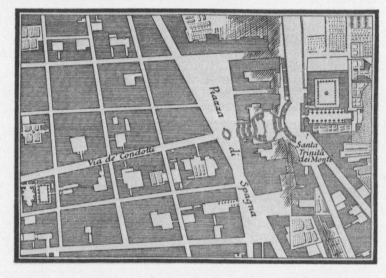

Left, an engraving of the Piazza di Spagna, made in 1750 by the architect Piranesi, showing the Spanish Steps and the Barcaccia fountain.

Below left, a temporary monument in honor of the birth of the Infanta of Spain, erected in 1727 in the Piazza di Spagna. The piazza owes its name to the Spanish Embassy to the Holy See, which since 1647 has been located in a palace overlooking the square.

Below right, a plan of the Piazza di Spagna and nearby streets.

tificate, he initiated the decentralization of Rome and set the stage for its future growth. Sixtus envisioned Rome as a system of straight arteries slicing through the network of medieval streets and linking the major pilgrimage churches of the city. Inspired by the spirit of the Counter Reformation, he believed that it was his calling to transform Rome into a magnificent, modern Christian city for the glory of God, and he commissioned the architect Domenico Fontana (1543–1607) to work on this project.

One of the most important streets and the first to get under way was the Strada Felice, now called the Via Sistina, leading from the church of Santa Maria Mag-

giore—more or less at the center of Sixtus's proposed network—to Trinità dei Monti. Little more of the plan was accomplished for some time, however, for Sixtus died in 1590, and the architect Fontana emigrated to Naples when he lost favor in the new papal court.

Thirty years later, during Urban VIII's papacy (1623–1644), architectural activity recommenced. Urban chose as his architect Gianlorenzo Bernini (1598–1680). Like Michelangelo before him, Bernini excelled as architect, painter, and poet, but felt himself to be a sculptor above all else. He was a man of deep religious faith, charming and aristocratic, a stable and steady worker who created rapidly and

with ease. Bernini endowed Rome with a number of masterpieces, including the dramatic colonnade of the Piazza of St. Peter's.

Historians are divided over whether the Barcaccia fountain in the Piazza di Spagna is the work of Bernini's father or an early work by the sculptor himself. In 1625, Urban VIII had restored the Aqua Vergine aqueduct—originally built by Agrippa in 19 B.C.—and in 1627, pipes were set in place for a fountain. The Barcaccia, in the form of a low, wide marble ship, was completed two years later and is the focal point of the piazza. Because of low water pressure in the area, the ship was designed to spout water gently from decorative suns and portholes at both ends and from a central spout that splashes water down into the body of the ship. The "old tub," as Romans call it, seems stranded in an oval pond just large enough to contain it. The fountain is actually a complex Baroque sculptural form, embodying a number of symbols in a fusion of fantasy and Counter-Reformation propaganda. The Barcaccia can be seen as a symbol of the Church Everlasting: Though constantly attacked by enemies of the faith, it does not sink.

The Piazza di Spagna is formed by two triangular spaces joined at their apexes. The Barcaccia is situated at that juncture, on the axis of the Via Condotti. In the seventeenth century, a number of imposing palaces on the piazza were built or restored by celebrated Baroque architects. From 1642 to 1644, Gianlorenzo Bernini oversaw the modernization of the façade of the Palazzo di Propaganda Fide (Propagation of the Faith) at the southern end of the Piazza di Spagna. Earlier, in 1634, Bernini had built a chapel, the Re Magi, inside the palace.

After the death of Urban VIII, Francesco Borromini, Bernini's greatest rival, took over the work on the palazzo. Borromini was a violent and erratic character who found the act of creation an agonizing struggle and eventually committed suicide. Nevertheless, he was a far more innovative architect than Bernini, introducing new and exciting spatial solutions in his designs and contributing as much as any architect since Michelangelo to the overthrow of the classically balanced Renaissance conception of architecture.

At the other end of the Piazza di Spagna, the architect Antonio del Grande began construction in 1647 on the fortresslike residence of the Spanish ambassador to the Holy See. This massive building added to the growing prestige and importance of the area. Yet Trinità dei Monti was still reached from the piazza with some difficulty, by means of a couple of steep, tree-lined dirt roads.

The idea of a monumental stairway leading from the piazza to Trinità dei Monti was first proposed by Cardinal Mazarin, the minister of King Louis XIV of France, and in 1660, the French attaché in Rome bequeathed a substantial sum of money to construct the stairway. Unfortunately Mazarin died at about the same time, and nothing was done until some sixty years later, when Pope Innocent XIII took an interest in the project. The pope chose a design for a stairway by the Architect Francesco De Sanctis (1693–1731). Work was begun in 1723 and completed in 1726.

De Sanctis considered three problems to be of fundamental importance. First, he wanted the stairway "to be in full view and open in all its parts in such a way that anyone beginning to ascend could see freely the whole way up to its top step." This was not only for aesthetic reasons but to discourage robbery and other "disturbances and unpleasantnesses."

Second, De Sanctis wanted the stairway to incorporate the symbolism and name of the church, Trinità dei Monti. "This is accomplished by beginning with three steps and their landing, from which lead up three curved stairs divided by benches, and each of these three stairs is divided into three equal flights. . . . All these flights lead up to a single large stairway at the center. . . . This stairway then separates into three ramps divided each into three flights. . . . In the center of this staircase has been formed a noble piazza, raised up, open and in full view, with its benches and its obelisk at the center. . . ."

De Sanctis's proposed obelisk was never erected, and balustrades were built instead of the planned benches. His third wish, to

Pope Urban VIII (below left) was the patron of Bernini (center) who worked on the Palazzo di Propaganda Fide (1642–1644) until he was replaced by Francesco Borromini, caricatured here (right) by the architect Domenico Fontana.

Bottom, an engraving by Piranesi looking toward the Palazzo di Propaganda Fide.

create "an inviting place that will offer utmost repose to the people," was fulfilled, with the exception of the flanking double row of trees he had planned. These trees were to have provided both visual harmony and shade, so that people could sit and rest out of the heat of the sun. In this, as in his overall design, De Sanctis was motivated by concern for the people who would use the staircase. And indeed, the honey-colored travertine steps and the sitting areas seem to be completed by the presence of people moving or resting on them.

The final addition to the steps was the granite obelisk, forty-four feet high, placed on a pedestal in front of Trinità dei Monti in 1788 by Pope Pius XI.

Today tourists ascending the gentle incline of steps, which open like a fan before them, come upon flower sellers, artists at work, and craftspeople with their wares spread out temptingly. Below, along the streets leading from the piazza, fashionable shops offer antiques, fine linen and lingerie, jewelry, and other luxuries. Around the corner from the piazza is the

Via Margutta, which has been long famous for its artists' studios and gardens.

Still a popular rendezvous is the famous Caffè Greco at 86 Via Condotti that opened soon after the Spanish Steps were built. The café was once a meeting place for artists and writers both Roman and foreign. Baudelaire, the Brownings, Goethe, and Gogol were just a few of its famous patrons. Another tradition is Babington's Tea Room at 23 Piazza di Spagna, which continues to cater to the needs of English tourists as it has since the eighteenth century. The signs for "waffles" and "hot cakes" in its windows indicate that

these days it is popular with American visitors as well.

The heritage of the past is preserved in Rome, the Eternal City. Yet the city is not a museum. Its monuments and buildings belong to the present more than to the past, for they are used and enjoyed by modern-day Romans. The Spanish Steps have lost none of their magical attraction. The aesthetes, bohemians, and intellectuals who frequented them in the eighteenth century have given way to students in blue jeans, curious visitors, and anyone else with time to stop and watch the world go by.

Right, a watercolor by Goethe of the Villa Medici in the foreign quarter of Rome. In 1803, the villa was purchased by Napoleon for use by those artists who had won the prestigious Prix de Rome. Among those who have stayed there were the composers Berlioz and Debussy and the architects Labrouste and Garnier.

Above, the English Romantic poet, John Keats, who died in a small room that looked out onto the Spanish Steps. Left, a nineteenth-century print of the Spanish Steps and the Barcaccia. The house where Keats lived is to the right of the stairs. It is now a museum dedicated to Keats and Shelley and contains memorabilia from nineteenth-century Rome.

Maharanah's Palace of Udaipur

India

The focal point of the city Udaipur, in the modern Indian state of Rajasthan, is the palace of the maharanah overlooking Lake Pichola (preceding page). On the far left is part of the original structure begun in 1567 by the Maharanah Udai Singh, founder of Udaipur. The main structure, on its right, with a profusion of arcades, towers, domes, and intricate windows, has been progressively enlarged by successive ranas (maharanahs) over the past four centuries; yet, the palace as a whole is remarkably harmonious and integrated.

The ghat (steps) (above left) descending to the lake allowed for easy embarkation onto the maharanah's boats. Sailing on the lake was his privilege and he alone owned boats. Below left, the original, late sixteenth-century palace buildings. Right, the elaborate, early seventeenth-century towers of the Rawala, or women's quarters, contrasting with the stark, heavy lower stories. Above, one of the delicate towers of the Bari Mahal, built in 1597. The original wing was built of thin slabs of rough sandstone, finely whitewashed to resemble the lavish marble surfaces of the court of the Mogul emperor at Delhi. In the seventeenth century, Udaipur's rana engaged architects from the imperial court at Delhi, who incorporated new harmony, balance, and elegance into the rather provincial Mewar architecture. Marble was extensively used in the Rawala complex. Delicate stone latticework and trellises relieved plain mural surfaces and admitted light and air while insuring privacy.

The section of the palace known as the Kusch Mahal (above left) was built in the early seventeenth century, when Udaipur began to flourish in an era of peace. Its abundant decorations, inspired by medieval Hindu forms, reflect the artistic renaissance of Udaipur. The superimposed, open galleries not only become smaller and more elegant from one story to the next, but also make the transition from post and lintel construction to an arcade in three subtle stages.

Left, the eastern façade of the Bari Mahal. In this part of the rana's palace, balconies, galleries, decorated roofs, brightly patterned tiles, and marble trellises are juxtaposed and interlaced in a harmonious complexity.

Lake Pichola (top right), constructed by means of dams and dikes in the fifteenth century, covers several square miles on the west side of Udaipur. Water drawn from the lake irrigates the city's gardens. On an island in the lake stands Jagniwas Palace, built as a summer residence in the mid-seventeenth century and now converted into one of the most luxurious—and most Indian— hotels in India.

Center right and below near right, the enclosed roof-top court of the Bari Mahal, overlooking the city of Udaipur and the Aravalli mountain range. Below far right, the Tripolia Gate, one of the three entrances to the palace. Above it, encircling the Bari Mahal, is a marble stringcourse of elephants in bas-relief.

During the early eighteenth century, open gardens were built on the roof of the Bari Mahal (left, top and center), embellished with the refinements of north Indian architecture: turrets, kiosks, pavilions, and trellises. The arched pavilions that punctuate the trellised walls afford clear views over the city and beyond. Below, one of the stucco elephants that guard the access to the lake. The elephant, a symbol of power and dominance, was extensively used in war.

Bottom left, gods of the Hindu pantheon. The Hindu faith was deeply rooted in Mewar, of which Udaipur became the capital after 1567. The Mewars considered themselves to be the elite descendants of a special princely warrior class, and it was this consciousness that spurred them in their bitter resistance to Mogul invaders.

Right, a view to the north from the upper story of the palace, showing the city of Udaipur and the central portion of the Tripolia Gate, built in 1711. The tiles clearly reflect the Moslem influence which began with the Moslem invasions of the fourteenth century and intensified with the Mogul incursions. Neither this gate nor the two others, on the eastern and southern walls of the city, was ever substantially fortified.

Mogul ascendancy in northwest India brought about the synthesis of Indian and Moslem artistic forms, evident during the sixteenth and seventeenth centuries in the widespread Indian use of Moslem elements such as domes, arches, enameled tiles, and oriel windows. Both traditions shared an interest in nature, luxury, and ordered calm, as well as in warlike activities. This Indo-Islamic style appears in the portrayal of a richly dressed Rajput noble on horseback (below far left) and another enjoying his water pipe (below near left). Magnificent glass mosaic peacocks and intricate tile patterns (center far left and near left), along with the liberal use of mirrors and frescoes (this page), created an atmosphere of princely opulence.

Maharanah's Palace of Udaipur India

The name India conjures up a collage of images in the Western mind: heat, dust, vast distances, exotic tropical vegetation, and spectacular monuments. Thoughts of its people call to mind opulence and poverty—a huge population born into an elaborate culture and a sophisticated religion.

India's great cities make an equally intense impression. The former colonial seaports of Calcutta and Bombay are both relatively worldly and cosmopolitan. Delhi, at the center of the interior's expanse, has the historical atmosphere of an ancient capital. Agra and Benares, with their remarkable memorials and religious structures, testify to the uniqueness of the Indian culture.

The fame of the city of Udaipur rests on another source—its architectural distinction and aristocratic tradition as a court city. It was the capital of Mewar, a princely state of old India. Today, it is part of Rajasthan, in the plains of northwestern India, some 200 miles from the Pakistan border. The princely states, some very large but most only a few square miles, were first formed in India's distant past. And many, like Mewar, continued under both British rule and the postcolonial republic until recent years. At that time, the central government in Delhi systematically abolished all the surviving princely titles and separate governments. Hence Udaipur has become a kind of living museum, lacking political significance, but rich in historical memories.

Only in the past two centuries has India become a recognizable political entity. Distance, natural obstacles, regional diversity, and the limitations of military technology had previously combined to encourage a feudal system of government like that of medieval Europe. As the British moved inland in the eighteenth century, they took into account the country's complex political structure. Most of India they governed directly. But they also reached agreements with many princely states. Keeping for themselves the control of defense, communications, and other matters affecting the whole of India, the British allowed the prince to rule his subjects as before. However, there was generally a British resident or agent in towns such as Udaipur, living discreetly in the background and reporting on all that transpired.

The British could also choose to act

Left, a map of northern India in the seventeenth century, at the height of the Mogul Empire. Udaipur lies in the southwestern part, between Gujurat (Guzurat) and Chitor. Above, the Mogul Emperor Aurangzeb (1658–1707), under whom the empire began to decline.

against gross misgovernment or independent princes. Ruling without legal restraints, the Indian sovereigns were regarded by their subjects virtually as demigods. Far from new political ideas, the princes sometimes degenerated into the cruelest of tyrants, indulging every whim or caprice. This sort of tyranny, however, is not recorded at Udaipur, whose reputation during the centuries of British rule has come down as that of a drowsy backwater.

The ruling house of Mewar traced its uninterrupted existence from the early eighth century. Legend projected its line even farther back to the god Rama, and through him to the sun itself. The founding of Udaipur as Mewar's capital in 1567 was one of the many consequences of the Mogul invasion of the early sixteenth century. The pattern of the invasion is a familiar one in Indian history. An adventurous Moslem chieftain named Babur from Central Asia, who was attracted by the wealth and fertility of an India weakened by internal dissension, launched his forces through the passes of the northwest frontier into Hindustan. Ambitious tribesmen, avid for loot, land, and slaves, flocked to Babur's banner with the first victories. He shaped them into a tightly disciplined force which, aided by artillery, defeated armies that were often far larger. Delhi was taken in 1540, and the other cities of

Above left, the fairytale palace of the ranas, rising above the city of Udaipur.

These two Mogul-style miniatures, dating from the late seventeenth century, illustrate a Hindu legend (above) and a love story (left).

northern India fell in rapid succession.

The name "Mogul" clearly derives from Mongol, but this is a misnomer. The invaders were mainly Turkish in origin, the heirs to a sophisticated culture that was centered in Samarkand and the oasis towns of Afghanistan and Uzbekistan. The Moguls, who readily adopted the cultural achievements of others, themselves could draw on an Islamic world that

stretched far to the west beyond Constantinople and Cairo to the Atlantic. Their delight in painting, poetry, architecture, and formal gardens left a distinctive mark on the states of northern India, including Rajasthan and Mewar.

At first the Moguls ran into some resistance in trying to conquer Mewar. The state's successive *ranas* (maharanahs or princes) embodied the traditions of independence and Hinduism. Unwilling to come to terms with the invaders, they gathered support from the other princes of Rajasthan. The Moguls, therefore, attacked Chitor, the capital of Mewar, in 1567. Before the siege lines tightened, the Rana Udai Singh fled with his court to a small valley in the hills some seventy miles away, and there Udaipur was founded.

Sitting in a niche on the eastern flank of the Aravalli hills at an altitude of some 2,500 feet, the new city of Udaipur had a natural defensive position. The hills rise steeply from the plains with several peaks reaching up about 3,000 feet. Crossed only by a few minor roads even today, these peaks hindered armies approaching on foot, camel, and ox cart from the northwest, the direct route from Central Asia. All across the broad belt of desert and arid country that lies across the present India-Pakistan border, food and water were scarce and artillery difficult to move.

There were further safeguards for the new city in the chain of lakes—some natural, some manmade—all interlocked with ditches and drainage canals that lay along the western boundary of Udaipur. The largest lakes are the Fateh Sagar and Lake Pichola. Two smaller ones, Sarup Sagar and Gobardhan Sagar, extend the chain. All these drastically limited the maneuverability of forces attacking from the west, while those coming from the east faced several rivers and a network of irrigation canals.

Within the large oblong formed by these water boundaries lay a long ridge, upon which Rana Udai Singh (after whom Udaipur is named) built the first small palace in 1567. Courtiers, tradesmen, and artisans began building nearby, and a small town was quickly established. These early buildings were constructed in a plain and undistinguished provincial style. Parts of them still survive: the Rai Angam Court (1571), the lower portions of a wing of the rana's palace, the arcades of the bazaar, and several other structures.

At that time and later on, Mewar's military architects stubbornly followed traditional models, refusing to modify their practices despite the siege artillery which

Right, festivities at the court of the Emperor Akbar (1542–1605), during whose reign the Mogul Empire flourished, culturally as well as militarily. Under Akbar, much of northern India was not only conquered but also politically stabilized and consolidated.

Below, a Mogul miniature portraying a nobleman about to strike down a rooster whose cries at dawn threaten to awaken his wife. This scene unconsciously illustrates the frequent refusal of Rajput and Mogul alike to acknowledge unpleasant reality, emphasizing their unrealistic desire to remain in a dream world.

the Moguls employed so successfully. Hence the high, narrow walls and towers of Udaipur presented an inviting target.

Udaipur stagnated artistically until the early seventeenth century, as the successive ranas of Mewar waged bitter wars against overwhelming Mogul power. Udaipur was captured by the Moguls and then restored to the rana. Mewar suffered severely while it watched the other states of Rajasthan begin accepting Mogul rule and Mogul artistic styles. The cycle of wars ended in 1614, when Udaipur's Rana Amar Singh finally accepted fairly generous peace terms from the Moguls and recognized their sovereignty.

Signs of an artistic revival had appeared in Udaipur some years earlier, with the construction of several Hindu temples, a large palace gate, and the small palace of Amar Mahal on Lake Pichola. But it was only when peace was established, and especially during the 1620s under Rana Karan Singh, that the revival blossomed.

Karan Singh had been much influenced by Mogul culture and advocated peace and harmony between Hindus and Moslems. He gave Udaipur a new grandeur and artistic significance by enlarging Lake Pichola, constructing the fortified ring of walls and elaborate gates that still stands, building up the old palace into a royal structure, and adding the Rawala, a huge block of rooms embellished with towers and trellised balconies for the court women. The rana also began the Jagmandir Palace on an island in Lake Pichola which was completed by his successor, the Rana Jagat Singh (1628–1652). During this reign, the royal palace was also finished, and the first stones were laid for yet another palace—Jagniwas—on a second island in Lake Pichola.

Outstanding among the structures built under Jagat Singh was the Jagannath Temple, completed in 1652, which stands near the rana's palace. Though the temple bore on its walls the usual panels depicting gods and goddesses, it also demonstrated the more secular Rajput style that had been developing for two centuries or more: animal and human friezes that show horsemen, elephants and their riders, dancers, processions of various sorts, and other dynamic, human scenes. These images are certainly not literal or naturalistic, but they evoke nonetheless a sensitivity for portraits from daily life.

The palaces of Udaipur equaled those elsewhere in northern India in luxury and sophistication. An ancient yet vigorous culture had established definite behavioral traditions, which were reflected in the explicit functions of separate rooms and apartments in the buildings. There were rooms for ceremonies, dining, conversation, dressing, bathing, and sleeping—the bedrooms often opening onto enclosed courtyards. Latticed and trellised balconies provided both privacy and fresh air, while high ceilings and thick stone walls helped to keep the interiors cool.

Furniture was sparse, mainly consisting of opulent cushions and rugs. Walls were often ornamented with paintings or inlaid with ceramics and precious stone. These luxuries were matched in Udaipur by the city's abundance of water. This ultimate necessity in the arid world of northwest India could—almost—be taken for granted in Udaipur. There was water for baths, fountains, lakes, irrigation canals, and gardens.

Udaipur entered a new phase during the late seventeenth century, as friction increased with the Moguls. The tolerance with which earlier Mogul leaders had viewed the Hindu vassal states was eroding. The Hindus, particularly those of Rajasthan, responded by preparing for war, which did indeed begin in 1678. Mewar more than held its own, defeating several invading Mogul armies. Udaipur was temporarily captured, but the city was not damaged.

By the early eighteenth century, the decline of the Mogul Empire had given the princes of Mewar a chance to reassert their sovereignty. They further expressed their energies in a new building campaign. Additions were made to the rana's palace and to the small palace on Jagmandir Island. The Tripolia Gate was cut into the city walls, and the Jagniwas Palace was finally finished on its island in Lake Pichola.

During the sixteenth to the eighteenth centuries, the rulers of Mewar left their mark on the architectural heritage of Udaipur. The architects and artisans they employed were neither particularly innovative nor individualistic, and their work remains anonymous. But they functioned within an artistic tradition that encouraged fantasy, extravagance, and splendor—the qualities that Western realism often avoids—making the city of Udaipur all the more exotic and delightful in the eyes of the West.

Left, the maharani's birthday parade through Udaipur—when there still were maharanis. The towers and turrets of the royal palace rise in the background.

Beautiful Lake Pichola (right), beside which Udaipur is built, is a life-giving source of water. The poorer inhabitants still transport the water in huge vessels.

Chateau
of Azay-le-Rideau

Loire Valley, France

The chateau of Azay-le-Rideau, built in the middle of the Indre River in France's famous Loire Valley, is a medieval fortress transformed during the Renaissance into a stately country manor. It was among several such feudal castles refashioned as pleasure estates as the valley evolved from a royal battleground to a royal playground in the early sixteenth century. Old castles were favored sites because the same features that made them militarily favorable—rising towers, surrounding water—were also picturesque emblems of their new owners' prestige.

In the morning stillness, Azay-le-Rideau is mirrored in the reflective moat surrounding the western façade (preceding page). The original fortified castle on the site was built in the early thirteenth century by Hugues-le-Ridel, a knight in the service of King Philip II Augustus. Burned in 1418 by the angered dauphin (later Charles VII), the chateau was carefully rebuilt one hundred years later by Gilles Berthelot, a prosperous banker, and his wife, Philippe. At Azay, the traditional medieval defensive elements have been transformed. The sentry walk, for example, is now an enclosed gallery.

Right, the southern façade of Azay-le-Rideau, reflected in the Indre. A Gothic influence survives in the castle's turrets and machicolations, while the Renaissance is reflected in the sculptural reliefs, the predominant horizontal moldings, and the pilasters framing the windows.

The main entrance of the chateau on its northern façade (above left) is a twin, arched portal surmounted by three pairs of arched windows on the stair landings. Before it stretches the court of honor, bounded on two sides by the building and on the other two by water (a variation on the typically enclosed Gothic court). The moat in front of the castle, which is, in fact, a branch of the Indre, is marked by a row of bushes at the far edge of the lawn. Azay-le-Rideau has an unusual, L-shaped plan, with its longer section facing the river. Below left, the eastern end of the chateau.

While retaining a basically Gothic profile, the gable crowning the main entrance (top far left) houses two Renaissance arches framed by pilasters. The symmetrical main entrance (top right) leads inside to the innovative royal staircase built with straight flights of stairs instead of the traditional spiral shape. The salamander and the ermine carved just below the top entrance gable (bottom far left) were the personal insignias of King François I and Queen Claude. The seventeen dormer windows (center far left) enliven the chateau's roofline with vertical accents. The corner turrets at Azay (near left) continue the military decorative motif. Keyhole windows, such as those located between the square upper-story windows, originally would have enabled medieval defenders to pour boiling oil onto their attackers below, but in Azay they are purely ornamental. Above, a carved scallop shell decorating a tower door.

The corner foundations of Azay (top left) rise naturally out of the Indre into a series of rounded moldings which, in turn, become the chateau's corner turrets. The ivy-covered castellated wall along the moat (center left) blends easily with its natural surroundings. Among the seventeenth-century additions to the chateau are the servants' quarters next to the entrance (bottom left) and the Lord's Chapel (above).

Inside the chateau, both French Gothic and Italian Renaissance elements mingle in the ceiling over the royal staircase. For example, the rosettes in the ceiling above the landing (above right) and the portrait medallions (near right) of the kings and queens of France, from Louis XI (1423–1483) to Henry IV (1553–1610), illustrate the Italian influence. The pendants and moldings surrounding the rosettes and medallions reflect a French Gothic spirit.

The kitchen at Azay (bottom far right) with its great fireplace now displays Renaissance furnishings and cooking utensils. Center far right, the façade of the twelfth-century church of Saint Symphorien in the small village of Azay near the chateau. The Romanesque sculpture of Christ among the disciples is interrupted by a Gothic stained-glass window dating from the thirteenth century.

Huge Renaissance fireplaces—a luxury at the time they were built—dominate the interiors of Azay-le-Rideau, particularly the dining room (above left). This room, it is said, was the scene of a near tragedy during the Franco-Prussian War in 1870 when the chandelier fell, just missing Prince Frederick Charles of Prussia. Suspecting an assassination attempt, the prince ordered the chateau burned immediately but rescinded the command when the incident was proven accidental. Above center, the royal bedchamber used by Bourbon kings during their visits to the chateau. The Yellow Room (above far right) and the Red Room (below), so named because of their wall hangings, are today furnished with sixteenth- and seventeenth-century pieces. The portrait on the far wall of the Red Room is of Gabrielle d'Estrées, mistress of Henry IV. Among the masterpieces found at Azay are the Gobelins tapestry (near right) in the Great Hall which depicts scenes of French country life and a writing desk (center far right) with decorative panels illustrating the miseries of war (bottom far right).

Chateau of Azay-le-Rideau Loire Valley, France

Every traveler—and Frenchman—has his favorite region in France. The orchards of Brittany, the elegant Parisian boulevards, the pine-scented villages of the Riviera, and the Jura Mountains carpeted with summer wildflowers all have their devotees. One of the most popular areas, among foreigners and Frenchmen alike, is the Loire Valley. Dotted with chateaux dating from the Middle Ages, this fertile valley epitomizes the long heritage of French civilization and history.

One of the oldest and most magical of the Loire Valley chateaux is Azay-le-Rideau. A graceful and delicate fairy palace framed by foliage and reflected in the placid water of the Indre River, the chateau stands at the junction of two cultural and architectural traditions: the waning Gothic and the ascending Renaissance.

The history of the chateau begins early in the thirteenth century, during the reign of Philip II, whose political astuteness earned him the admiring epithet Augustus, after the greatest of the ancient Roman emperors. Early in his reign he consolidated his own power at the expense of his feudal lords. He took part in the Third Crusade, until he quarreled with Richard I of England and returned to France. He then turned problems closer to home into victories, defeating the alliance of England, the Holy Roman Empire, and Flanders and winning back valuable French domains from England's King John. Philip established France as a lead-ing European power and initiated important reforms within his own kingdom.

Among the domains regained from the English was the province of Touraine. This beautiful region, which includes the Loire Valley with its luxuriant vineyards and orchards, is known as "the garden of France." It was bitterly contested by England and France, and numerous chateaux—among them Azay-le-Rideau, Chinon, and Amboise—were built to defend the area.

Among the subjects knighted by Philip for faithful service was one Hugues-le-Ridel, or Rideau, who then built a strongly fortified castle at Azay on an island in the Indre River, a tributary of the Loire. The castle, which became known as Azay-le-Rideau, was strategically important. To the north lay the ancient and powerful city

Below, an early nineteenth-century print showing the shorter ancient tower, said to date from the original thirteenth-century chateau, before it was replaced by a tower matching the others.

Charles VII (near left) burned the original fortress of Azay-le-Rideau (1418) because the Burgundian troops occupying the chateau heckled him. Francis I (far left) confiscated the reconstructed chateau after its owner, Gilles Berthelot, fled France in the wake of a political and financial scandal. Francis was an enthusiastic proponent of the Italian Renaissance and introduced Italian ideas and fashions into France.

of Tours, capital of the region; almost equidistant to the south lay the stronghold of Chinon, perched on its peak overlooking the Loire and Vienne rivers.

Two centuries later, the English and their Burgundian allies again occupied the entire northern half of France down to the Loire. The rest of France was ruled by Charles VI, whose son was known as "Charles the Indolent" on account of his political ineffectiveness and profligate personal life. (Later, however, Joan of Arc was to transform this unlikely candidate into Charles VII—"the Well-Served"—by leading his army against the English and raising the siege of Orléans.) As Charles the Indolent passed by the chateau of Azay-le-Rideau in 1418, he was greeted by the laughter and jeers of the Burgundians occupying the chateau. In response, Charles stormed the castle, hanged the whole garrison of 345 men, and burned the building. Throughout the next century it was known, even in official documents, as Azay-le-Brûlé—Azay the Burned.

Later, Jean Berthelot, the mayor of Tours, bought the ruined chateau. When his son Gilles inherited it, he ordered its

reconstruction. And from 1518 to 1529, as many as 120 men labored under the direction of master mason Etienne Rousseau to turn the chateau into a splendid palace.

Unlike the first builder of Azay, Gilles Berthelot was not a warrior knight but the vastly wealthy treasurer general of France and master of the chamber of accounts of Paris. A prominent figure at the court of King Francis I (1494–1547), he was also related to the other great financier families of Anjou and Touraine who were transforming the now-peaceful Loire Valley into a region of country estates and castles. In 1515, Thomas Bohiers and his wife Catherine Briçonnet had begun the splendid chateau of Chenonceaux on the site of an old mill, and at about the same time Florimond Robertet began to build the chateau at Bury.

Even though Etienne Rousseau was nominally the director of operations, Azay reflects the taste of Berthelot's wife, Philippe Lesbahy. Architecturally and artistically inclined, Philippe also had the organizing ability and the ambition to make her wishes come true.

But Philippe and her husband were un-

able to enjoy their architectural marvel for long. Implicated in a political and financial scandal that sent to the scaffold one of Gilles Berthelot's cousins by marriage, they fled France, never to return. The king, Francis I, confiscated the estate and gave it to one of his favorites, Antoine Raffin, captain of the Royal Guard. Raffin became the first of many owners.

No fundamental modifications were made to the chateau until the nineteenth century, when it was extensively restored and rebuilt. Unfortunately, this included the elimination of an ancient tower to the right of the entrance court, which was said to have dated from the time of Hugues-le-Ridel. It was replaced by a tower in the style of the rest of the building. A narrow tower to the left of the entrance court, which was said to detract from the symmetry of the building, was also replaced.

Azay-le-Rideau is no longer a private residence. In 1901, the furnishings were shipped to Paris for auction. In 1905, the chateau was bought by the state. It is now a museum of Renaissance furnishings.

When Hugues-le-Ridel was master of Azay, the entire family, including servants and retainers, lived in one room above the entrance to the main keep. For protection, the ladder by which they entered would be drawn up after them. Later, at the time Azay was reconstructed, life became more peaceful and enjoyable, and chateau owners became influenced by the ideas of comfort and luxury that the Crusaders brought back from the East.

In most chateaux, a separate chamber, the Great Hall, was set aside for public audiences and feasts. Private family life and private entertaining were conducted in the room, which tended to become increasingly richly furnished. Smaller rooms

Above, detail of a drawing showing the royal portal at Azay-le-Rideau. Below left, the façade of the parallel staircase at Azay, and below right, the famous exposed spiral staircase at Blois, the residence of Francis I. The wing that Francis built at Blois established the Italian Renaissance style in France.

adjoining the main room served as audience chambers, a chapel, and as workrooms for servants. A separate kitchen came into general use. In the great royal houses, there was also a robing room which contained a very ornate bed and various ceremonial garments. After partially dressing himself in the main room among his family, the lord of the chateau would complete his toilet before a different audience. This custom was the origin of the famous *petites* and *grandes levées* which Louis XIV later developed at Versailles.

Standards of personal hygiene were relatively high before the fourteenth century. Medieval castles were well supplied with conveniences, and their occupants often bathed daily, while the common people visited public baths as often as once a week. After the fourteenth century there was a decline of cleanliness and hygiene, probably encouraged by the clergy who advocated mortification of the flesh and deplored the debauchery of the public baths.

Checkers, dice, chess, and cards were popular pastimes among those who lived in chateaux. Outdoors, men played bowls, softball, and tennis and practiced archery and wrestling. The nobility also amused themselves with tournaments and hunting. Women and children were entertained by dwarfs; the court jester mocked everyone, from highest to lowest. Festivals, balls, banquets, and masquerades were held frequently, and the appearance of a group of wandering minstrels or mystery players provided a welcome impromptu diversion.

During the first half of the sixteenth century, the armies of France and the Holy Roman Empire were disputing their rival claims to supremacy in Italy. The influence of the Italian Renaissance—then at its height—was brought home to France by Francis I, who loved luxury and all things Italian. The French people eagerly followed his lead. Released from the austere

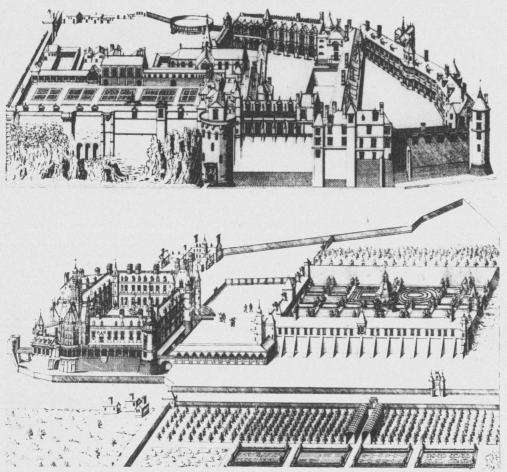

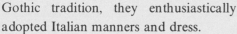

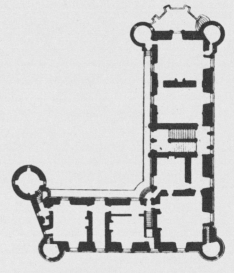

Above left, the chateau of Amboise as it appeared in the sixteenth century. Here Leonardo da Vinci died. Left, the chateau of Gaillard, originally built by Richard I of England at the same time as the original Azay-le-Rideau. Above, the plan of the ground floor of Azay-le-Rideau. One of the wings is built out over the river, and there is a forecourt at the angle of the L.

Gothic tradition, they enthusiastically adopted Italian manners and dress.

The young and vigorous Francis also set the fashions in the Loire Valley, transforming it from a battleground into a royal playground. He turned his attention to the ancient chateau at Blois, which his predecessor Louis XII had made the official royal residence. The wing that Francis built at Blois became the touchstone for architectural style throughout France.

Philippe Lesbahy emulated this style—no longer Gothic, yet not fully Renaissance—at Azay-le-Rideau. The chateau of Azay is unusual in that it is L-shaped. The western wing stands on dry land, while the southern wing is built up out of the river. There is no historical record of any intention to build further wings to enclose the courtyard. An irregular ground plan was not unusual in the Middle Ages, although it was—in theory, at any rate—rejected by the Renaissance. Besides, the builders were using the existing foundations on a very difficult site.

One of Azay-le-Rideau's main innovations, derived from the Italian Renaissance, is the central staircase. Rather than the traditional tight Gothic spiral staircase, Azay-le-Rideau boasts one of the first monumental straight staircases in France. Four stories high, its flights, which are separated by a wall, run parallel to each other. The staircase is emphasized on the outer wall of the northern façade by the pairs of open arches which illuminate its intermediate landings. These are surmounted by an elaborate ornamental gable and flanked by Classical columns, sometimes alternating with elongated niches. Above the flights of stairs, its vaulted ceiling is composed of a grid of Gothic-style moldings, forming hanging pendants at the intersections and enclosing portrait medallions of all the kings of France from Louis XI to Henry IV. The influence of the Renaissance is also evident in the more comfortable and luxurious arrangement of the interior rooms.

On the outer walls, the pilasters and stringcourses (the narrow horizontal moldings which continue the lines of the windowsills and lintels) further reflect Renaissance taste, while the very ornate gables on all the dormer windows projecting above the cornice line are another Gothic feature restated in Italian terms. Elsewhere, medieval elements have been reduced to ornamentation. The crenelations have been transformed into the windows of an inside corridor linking the rooms on the top floor. The machicolations, through which, in an earlier age, boiling oil would have been poured on assailants below, are still present. They were no longer required to serve any defensive purpose, for projecting ornamental stringcourses, which would have afforded shelter to any attacker below, were built beneath them. The towers have become graceful turrets with pepper-pot roofs and lacy ornaments. But it is in its large windows that the chateau most differs from earlier fortified castles.

At Azay-le-Rideau, Gothic might has given way to Renaissance grace, and the last vestiges of an earlier day serve only to accentuate the new style. Indeed, the obviously nonfunctional character of the towers and battlements lends to Azay-le-Rideau the quality of an enchanted palace. The medieval castle of war has become an elegant residence of the Renaissance.

Casino at Deauville

France

The gambling casino at Deauville, on the Channel coast of France (preceding page and these pages), enjoyed its greatest fame during the 1920s as a playground for some of the wealthiest men in the world. One of them, André Citroën, the French automobile manufacturer, expressed his widely shared attraction to gambling at Deauville: "I'm not the least interested in the game," he once said, "nor in whether I win or lose. I am only interested in whether or not the amount is large enough to be noticed." The casualness with which millionaires, monarchs, and men-about-town staked huge sums on the turn of a card in Deauville's casino soon began to ripple through high society, even finding its way into the gossip columns of many international newspapers.

The gentlemen who were prepared to bet thousands of francs on a single card moved in tandem with a number of professional gamblers. The most famous of these were the so-called "Greek Syndicate" (of whom only three of the five were Greek). The ominous sound of the term "syndicate" is misleading. These men had no underworld or criminal connection of any kind. What they did have were unusual mathematical abilities, combined with remarkable coolness, style, and self-confidence. By joining forces, they each amassed sizable fortunes and soon adopted lifestyles like those of the wealthy men they regularly outplayed, season after season.

Baccarat was the favorite game, allowing anywhere between three and eleven people to play. Its complex rules and demand for a high level of concentration lent it much prestige among serious gamblers. For the more frivolous, the casino also offered boule—a kind of roulette played for relatively low stakes—which was highly patronized by the elderly and day trippers.

In its architecture, the casino (details on these pages) typifies the Neoclassical revival, with its concern for dignity and grandeur, which emerged during the years just before World War I. Rebuilt in the Louis XVI style in 1912, the casino contrasts curiously with what Deauville became in the twenties, when skirts shortened, bathing suits grew skimpier, and the traditional conventions of good behavior were overturned.

The Deauville casino suggests an elegance and refinement somewhat at odds with the tasteless squandering of money indulged in by the nouveaux riches during the heyday of the town. The rather insipid neo-Baroque sculptures on these pages wait patiently for the beginning of the "season" at Deauville—August 1. Suddenly, the quiet town of 5,000 people is invaded by the 50,000 visitors who regularly flock to the internationally popular resort.

Upon entering the casino, gamblers in the twenties encountered two nuns with offertory plates, who often collected substantial sums during a busy evening. The visitor then entered a huge square hall containing a dance band and boule tables (below left). The band played around the clock, as did the boule players; but their efforts were not taken seriously, either by the management or by other gamblers. Beyond was the heart of the casino: the restaurant and, above all, the rooms for baccarat and chemin de fer—a variant of baccarat. Those who wished to join the players had to pay an entrance fee and be scrutinized—politely but thoroughly—by the physiognomist. The casino maintained a file of cheats and other undesirables who were refused admission if the physiognomist identified them at the door. Among the latter were those known to cause trouble or disturb other players by indiscreet behavior. Even today, the casino wishes to avoid scandal and will go to any length to prevent suicides, brawls, or spectacular unrecoupable losses.

The tables enclosed by brass railings (above right and below far right) are for big-time baccarat players. The minimum stakes are announced on the sign above the table. It is hard to cheat at baccarat, and the casino takes various security measures to make it even more difficult. Some chips, for example, glow when placed under ultraviolet light. Others are electromagnetically coded at the casino. Deauville's casino also has its own electricity generating system so that the lights will remain on, even if the town plunges into darkness.

Above left, the roulette table. Roulette was not played in the twenties, but today it is one of the most popular games.

Casino at Deauville France

A line of breakers rolls onto the wide beach. There are clumps of cabanas, umbrellas, folding chairs. A few bathers brave the cold of the English Channel. The town is a compact patch of substantial houses, a few rambling hotels, beautifully tended gardens, and quiet streets. Yachts rock on the sea, lending color to a scene often illustrated by Raoul Dufy, Kees van Dongen, and others.

This is Deauville. For eleven months of the year, it is a quiet town of 5,000 inhabitants, just one among many seasonal resorts on the Normandy coast. But each August it is transformed by an influx of the fashionable world, which flocks to gamble at the casino, to stroll on the boardwalk, to watch horse races and polo matches at the Hippodrome, and, above all, to see and be seen.

Deauville's pre-eminence dates back to the middle of the nineteenth century. Then, the social calendar of the French upper crust included the *petite saison,* which ran from December to Easter, followed by the *grande saison,* that lasted until mid-June. These months were generally passed in the city. Then the flight began to the French Alps or the seashore, Deauville in August being the most chic venue. The autumn was spent in the country at extended house parties in large chateaux. The cycle began again with the return to Paris in December.

During the season, the presence of an individual at a spot such as Deauville strengthened his or her claim to membership in "society." Through consorting with, say, a duke or a count, a factory owner came to be considered an industrialist, and a stock market speculator became known as a financier.

Deauville is well suited for bringing society together. It is small and select, and its limits are clearly defined. The Channel is to the west, the Hippodrome to the east, the hamlet of Bennerville by the cliffs to the south, and the River Touques to the north, separating the town from Trouville, its middle-class neighbor. Deauville's few streets follow a regular grid plan cut diagonally by several long boulevards that radiate outward from the town's hub at the Place Morny. Nearby is the railway station—in times past the vital connecting link to Paris, some 125 miles away. Now the affluent arrive by car or even by private plane. The Aga Kahn IV has been known to fly from his resort on Sardinia to witness a single race and then leave right after the finish.

Even today there are those so loyal that they claim to prefer Deauville, in season, to any other place in the world. For them there is a wide variety of amusements: golf, tennis, a bridge club of international renown, and a small theater. Discotheques and night clubs are also discreetly present, and, of course, there is year-round activity at the casino. Deauville may lack the notoriety of a Monte Carlo or a Las Vegas, but this accords with its own unobtrusive

Right, an early aerial view of Deauville. The Hippodrome is in the right foreground, the English Channel in the background, and the town of Trouville in the right background. Separating the two towns is the River Touques, whose banks are strengthened by breakwaters that reach into the Channel.

Far left and above, posters advertising the casinos at the nearby resorts of Dieppe and Le Tréport. Center top, Napoleon III, whose reign (1852–1871) saw the birth of Deauville at the hands of the Duc de Morny (1811–1865), his half brother (near left).

style. Yachting is among the more popular diversions: Deauville is the terminus of the annual race from Cowes on the Isle of Wight. But the huge floating mansions of the twenties have, for the most part, been replaced by smaller, more navigable craft, whose owners are less concerned with social prestige and entertaining.

Apart from providing recreation for yachtsmen, the sea plays a minor role in the Deauville season. It serves largely as an aesthetic backdrop or a playground for children; it is too cold, stormy, and inhospitable for the fashionable visitor. Tristan Bernard, a celebrated dramatist and boulevardier of the *belle époque* expressed it neatly: "I love Deauville—it's so close to Paris and so far from the sea." The Marquis Boni de Castelane, a pillar of Deauville society in the 1920s, would enter the water to swim a few strokes only after a footman with a large thermometer had ascertained the temperature.

Many of Deauville's habitués have bought houses in the town, usually modest villas in a vaguely Gothic or Tudor style. Flower beds and shrubbery, surrounded by low stucco walls, frequently grace the grounds. The furniture within is usually not grand—Deauville's concern with fashion stresses cars and clothing over houses and furniture.

Near the beach stand Deauville's few hotels, the heritage of the era just before World War I when the town was in its second heyday. The hotels are excellent— and expensive—and their private dining rooms are much in demand. Reservations for August are made many months in advance, causing difficulties for those who trust to their luck or influence to find accommodations at the last minute.

Eastern Normandy is fashionable horse-breeding country, and today it is racing that shapes Deauville's season, attracting American, British, and other foreign visitors, as well as flocks of day trippers from Paris. Racing also brings to Deauville detachments from the prestigious French Jockey Club.

Following English models, this club was founded in 1833 for the purpose of improving thoroughbred racing—although gastronomy and gambling soon became essential club activities also. Members included wealthy blue bloods as well as nonaristocrats—as long as they were sufficiently distinguished and stylish. Important foreigners (most notably, the future King Edward VII) were also members. Not surprisingly, this fashionable clientele took quickly to Deauville, with its facilities for racing and gambling.

The Duc de Morny, one of the most influential figures of the Second Empire of Napoleon III (1852–1871), was largely responsible for the fortunes of Deauville. Born in 1778, Morny was the illegitimate half brother of Napoleon III. Ambitious and energetic, charming and helpful when it seemed appropriate, he served as president of the legislature from 1856 onward. Morny spent lavishly on women, entertainment, horses, and clothing and dabbled in the stock market much as he manipulated the legislature. In both cases he showed a golden touch and served as an important link between the government and the rising class of entrepreneurs and speculators.

That monied world discovered the Channel coast in the 1850s, when the new railway system began to provide easy access to Dieppe and Fécamp in the east and to Trouville and Cabourg west of the Seine. France was then booming economically and changing socially. New fortunes were amassed in the wake of many ambitious undertakings—railways, the rebuilding of Paris, the Suez Canal—encouraged by Napoleon III. Scruples were cast aside in the race for wealth.

The idea of Deauville was born out of Morny's desire for a summer arena for horse racing in France, to compare with the then-fashionable Baden-Baden in Germany. He had already persuaded his half brother to build a winter course at Longchamp in Paris. In addition, Morny believed that his weak lungs might benefit from the Channel air.

In 1858, when Morny and some other investors began planning its expansion, Deauville consisted of only a few farmhouses. The duke's involvement reassured the cautious, while the ambitious grasped the opportunity to enter the inner circle of politics which Morny represented. In 1860, Morny's group bought some 300 acres of marsh and dunes. In 1861, a bridge was built across the Touques, linking Deauville and Trouville. The all-important rail connection to Paris was completed in 1863, and the Hippodrome hosted its first race in 1864, when Morny was feted with elaborate ceremonies worthy of a king.

Morny died very suddenly a year after the Hippodrome opened, and the Deauville boom soon slowed, virtually halting with the onset of the Franco-Prussian War in 1870. France was defeated, the leaders of the Second Empire dropped out of public life, and Deauville declined along with its clientele. The casino, closed in 1895, was demolished in 1902.

Under the auspices of Eugene Cor-

Daily life during the Deauville "season." Above, the bathing cabins from which nineteenth-century visitors braved the sea. Left, genteel recreation along the beach. Below, strollers observing social proprieties on promenades.

nuché, a revival began in 1912. Cornuché had commenced his career as a waiter in Paris and had soon taken over a fading restaurant called Maxime's (today the famous Maxim's). Later he had similar success with a restaurant and casino in Trouville. But Cornuché was irritated by the limitations imposed on him there, and in 1912, he crossed the Touques with a small band of investors to build a new, splendid casino at Deauville.

Virtually overnight, Deauville was reborn, with gambling for high stakes edging out racing as its principal attraction. The clientele Cornuché had developed at Maxime's followed him to Deauville each August. Two new hotels were built—just in time to be used as hospitals during World War I. All gambling was suspended until 1919.

The 1920s saw Deauville at the center of the fashionable world. If the German and Russian nobility had been eliminated financially by inflation and revolution respectively, the slack was more than taken up by wealthy luminaries and social groups that previously had made only oc-casional forays into European high society. Deauville's simple boardwalk now saw war profiteers from the industrial countries, kings from Scandinavia and Iberia, and potentates from the Middle East and India. There were flashy million-aires, like James Hennessy, the French brandy king, Gordon Selfridge, the British department store magnate, and André Citroën, the French automobile tycoon, whose gambling exploits kept them in the public eye.

These big spenders attracted a wide cir-cle of journalists and jockeys, wealthy widows and their gigolos, fanatical petty gamblers, and assorted swindlers. Some of the rich were known to be grandiose tip-pers; others were notoriously careful, even stingy. Baron Henri de Rothschild always wore the same old black hat and smoked the cheapest French cigarettes, protesting that, despite his fortune, he lacked ready cash.

Deauville also was alive with young women, who often combined remarkable beauty with straightforward cupidity. Deauville's excellent jewelers were avail-able to enhance the former and satisfy the latter. A rich man's mistress was as much a testimonial to his wealth as the money he lost each night at baccarat or chemin de fer.

The Deauville extravaganza began to tone down in the 1930s. Economic depres-sion, inquisitive tax collectors, and a changing social climate all helped impose discretion on the big spenders. World War II left the cliffs around Deauville dotted with the concrete bunkers of the German "Atlantic Wall," built to fend off the Al-lied invasion, which eventually came only a few miles down the beach. And postwar economic austerity decreed Deauville a sluggish revival.

Today governesses and family groups have replaced the spectacular and the fabulous on the promenades. Deauville has diversified its offerings and now caters also to the near-rich and the not-so-rich. Though the Duc de Morny and the big gamblers of the 1920s would perhaps be dismayed, Deauville has aged gracefully.

Left, a drawing by Félix Vallotton, de-picting the sea at Deauville—a suitable playground for women and children but not for grown men.